Mastering Google AdWords:

Step-by-Step Instructions for Advertising Your Business (Including Google Analytics)

Table of Contents

Introduction

The influence that Google wields on the world is immense. The odds are you probably use Google every day for various purposes. You might use it to get information on some retailer in your local area or maybe to learn new things. Perhaps you might be thinking of something and you need to get an answer so you go to Google to find it.

Google can be used anywhere. You can use it on your computer as well as any mobile devices you have. You could even get a Google Home machines plugged into your home and connected to a network.

Today you can take advantage of the massive reach that Google has by getting in touch with people through your own listing. You can create a listing that includes a distinct heading ad copy. This can help people notice your site making it easier for you to be noticed by the crowd. You can use traditional search engine marketing or optimization practices to help make your listing more visible. From creating a new ad on Google to improving upon how your landing page works, you can do many things to make your site easier more visible.

There is a big problem that many people come across when they are trying to make themselves noticeable on Google. This is because of the immense amount of competition. With billions of entries on Google, it can be easy for anyone to become lost.

This can be problematic for people who are trying to run their own businesses and make them stand out in some fashion. Regardless of how focused or specific your keywords might be, you might still struggle to make your site visible on Google. Even if you have a local focus, it can still be a challenge to stand out among other people in your local community who are using the same keywords.

The regular SEO practices that you use might not be enough. You might have done everything possible to make your site visible and easy to find, but your listing is still not showing up as well as you might have hoped. This is a huge problem if your competition becomes easier to spot and gets more attention than you.

The challenge to be visible on Google can be solved by using Google AdWords. This is a popular pay-per-click or PPC advertising solution that provides a simple approach to handling your Google content.

To make Google AdWords effective, you have to know what you are doing and how to do it. This guide will help you understand how to advertise on Google.

The points covered here focus on how Google AdWords can work for you. You will learn about using AdWords with the right keywords, getting a great copy to work for you, and learn how to budget for using AdWords.

This guide covers information on how to use AdWords on mobile devices. More people than ever are using mobile technology to access Google. It only makes sense to learn how AdWords can be used on such devices.

You might be concerned about the cost of being visible on Google, but you will see that you can get a greater profit as more prospective customers come to your site. AdWords is not only a smart solution for marketing but also something that will make your content visible.

An Important Note

The content listed in this guide focuses on using the new version of Google AdWords. In 2017, a new version of the AdWords interface was produced. The design was made to create a more immersive and easier to use experience.

The instructions listed in this guide focus on how you can use the new version of AdWords. This is the version that should be the default edition that you use.

You have the option to choose the older version of AdWords. However, it might be easier for you to use the newer version of AdWords as it offers a simple interface that is not complicated.

Chapter 1 – What Is Google AdWords?

Everyone is getting onto Google these days for various purposes. Some people use it to find information on local retailers while others use it for getting and sending emails. You probably have used Google a few times today or this week.

Today Google can work with more than just information. It can work to support businesses that want to get exposure. Google AdWords is a popular service that Google offers to help people get online and be visible.

Google has been running AdWords since 2000 as a service where people can pay to get online and make their posts more visible.

Understanding the Basic Concept

With Google AdWords, you pay to get a small bit of advertising copy displayed on Google. Specifically, your ad will be displayed in a prominent part of a Google search page. You pay for each click that someone uses on your site. In particular, the ad will appear when someone is searching for some content relating to a keyword that you have used.

The intention is to make your content more visible. By using AdWords, you are doing more than just creating an advertisement - you are getting that ad to be more noticeable. There is a cost to get your ad fast-tracked onto Google so more people can see this.

This is a popular pay-per-click advertising solution (PPC). It is so popular that it has become Google's largest profit driver. It is estimated that Google earns more than $50 billion a year from advertising. This helps Google to keep many of its functions operational. However, Google only collects money from those who create the best possible advertisements that stand out and have meaning and purpose.

If you search for something on Google, you are almost surely going to see an advertisement that was paid for through the AdWords system. To notice one of these ads:

1. Type in a keyword into Google.

2. A series of listings will appear at the top part of the site. These are the ads that certain groups will have paid for.

3. The ads will include specific content listing information on not only the name of the site but also what it sells.

4. It will also include some extra links that take you to other parts of a site. These include certain spaces that focus on specific topics or concepts that a business can support.

The simplicity of Google AdWords is an important point to notice. When you use Google AdWords, you will make your site more visible and attractive. This, in turn, makes people want to click on the link to visit your site and see what you have to offer. To understand how the AdWords system works, you have to understand the concept of PPC, the basis of AdWords.

How AdWords Has Changed Over the Years

Google started working on the AdWords system in 2000 as a monthly advertising service. The search engine originally ran advertising campaigns for people who sent out information with their membership fees. Over time, Google changed the platform of AdWords to create a self-service setup where users have more control over their marketing.

As AdWords became more popular, Google started to include more features in its AdWords system. These features included shopping listings, support for Google Maps and so forth. AdWords has been fully integrated into just about everything that Google has to offer.

Google has changed to include support for mobile devices as well. In fact, Google increased the limits that people can use for their daily budgets. People can use larger budget caps than ever before as more people are becoming reliant on Google and the competition has been increasing.

Everything that Google has done to change AdWords over the years has been with two intentions in mind. First, Google wants to make it easier for people to control their campaigns. Second, Google is helping to make the content on AdWords appear in more places. The number of searches on Google has increased to about 3.5 billion per day on average. Because Google received around 20 million searches per day in 2000, it would be an understatement to say that the search engine has become a big deal. AdWords makes it possible for people to get the most out of their searches by making marketing efforts a little easier to work with.

Understanding PPC

The pay-per-click or PPC setup is the foundation of Google AdWords. PPC is a popular form of online marketing where advertisers pay a certain amount of money each time that an ad is clicked. In other words, a website pays to get its content listed onto a search engine.

To do this, a business creates a new advertisement that will appear on a search engine. This includes a unique heading and description alongside other extensions or bits of data one wants to add. The advertisement is engineered to draw attention and possibly clicks. Besides, the advertisement will appear at the top of a search provided that the keyword matches.

This is the opposite of trying to use organic means to make a website visible. Those who wish to use PPC solutions have to create the best possible advertisements that are relevant and potentially intriguing to customers, as you will learn throughout this guide.

The total amount of money that a person might spend for a click onto a site can vary based on what one is willing to spend and the quality of the link. With PPC, it is possible for a site to get a decent return on its investment provided its website is built to encourage people to check something out. The most attractive and successful advertisements can be posted online with smaller charges. That is, a person might not spend as much on each click if the ad is of the best possible quality.

Let's say that a vacuum cleaner salesman has a website that he wants to promote. He might pay $3 for each click to his link. When a customer clicks on the link and buys something on his website or in his physical retail store, that salesman will make a sizable profit. In other words, it only cost $3 to get someone to buy a vacuum cleaner that might be worth hundreds of dollars.

With PPC, people can spend as much or as little as they want to get their content visible online. Best of all, people can create limits as to how much money they will spend every day, week or month on PPC efforts. This ensures that one's content will only cost a certain amount of money to promote. An ad will go offline when the monetary limit is reached, but what matters is that a business will have spread the word about something without having to spend lots of effort in the process.

You could consider PPC to be the fast-track toward getting noticed online. Instead of using traditional organic methods of making a site visible, you would spend money to get something to be more visible on Google. There are many reasons why a business would use PPC to get online:

- The competition for a keyword might be incredibly intense. You might have to use PPC tactics to become visible while marketing your work online.

- You might have a perfectly organized website, but you have nothing else to work with. Choosing your keywords within a new PPC campaign may be the best move.

- Maybe you might be trying to create a new advertising venture that goes well beyond just using traditional post ads. Working with a PPC could make your content more intriguing.

- Sometimes a business needs to be visible just to get people to notice what the company does. Many PPC ads are produced by smaller or newer companies that are desperately trying to make their businesses easier to spot.

- A business might have a very specific type of promotion to highlight. This might entail a special limited-time sale or the introduction of a new product or service. A PPC can operate with keywords that are linked to the new campaign.

PPC is a fascinating field of work to undertake. When working on a PPC project, you might notice that your work will be more visible than you ever expected.

What It Takes to Succeed

You might assume that just paying to get to the top of a listing would help you to succeed, but there is more to working with AdWords. In particular, AdWords requires you to follow many of the basic tenets of running a quality campaign.

There are many things that must be followed for your campaign to work:

1. Your campaign has to be properly organized with the appropriate keywords that are relevant to your content. You can adjust those keywords to highlight specific content.

2. The content of your advertisement is a necessity to review - how well your ads are laid out and how they stand out to the reader. Your ad needs to include more than just a clever message. It should also include a reason for someone to visit your site.

3. The bidding used should be reasonable but still enough to make your ad visible. Those who spend more on their ads will more likely get their ads to show up, but those who have top-quality ads might not have to spend as much. Look at your budget - you do not want your ads to be finished too quickly.

4. The ads should also include enough additional extensions and features that make people want to learn more. Whether it entails telling people to call you or to download your app, your ad can include extensions that reveal more about what you have to offer.

5. Everything has to be fine-tuned regularly to give you a better control. You will have to adjust the settings on

your AdWords setup on occasion. You will need to change them based on what ads are the most popular and what needs extra attention. You can use the Analytics features on your AdWords dashboard to see how well your campaign is running and if you need to change anything.

All of these points will be covered throughout this guide. You will be amazed at how well you can get an AdWords campaign to work for you.

Chapter 2 – How Google AdWords Works

Google AdWords is one of the unique solutions to use when promoting content. What goes into this program and how does it work?

To make Google AdWords functional and useful:

1. A business starts by entering in its own unique listing. This will contend with others getting onto AdWords. The listing should include all the details that you want to mention within a certain amount of space. The content can be as basic or elaborate as you want it to be.

2. The business can preview or review the content included in the listing. With the right extensions and other features, you can get an AdWords message to be very detailed and unique.

3. When a person searches for a certain keyword, Google will compare that keyword with the content of sites that are advertising on AdWords. If you type in the words "florist shop." Google will notice that you are trying to find flower stores and florists in your area.

4. Google will review a search based on the location. Google will identify your IP address and match it with florist shops in your area. For example, a person who lives in Cleveland will be redirected to results that are in the Cleveland area or a national retailer that serves the city. Meanwhile, someone in Boston will get results that feature florists in the Boston area.

5. The ad copy will also be reviewed to see how relevant that copy is to what you are trying to find. The ad copy needs to include details on everything that a retailer has to offer. The florist shop's copy can include details on the types of flowers including prices and promotions. The advertisement can be very detailed or just simple, but an ad with more content might be loaded first.

6. The value of the advertisement should also be considered. Those who pay more per click will be more likely to have their ads noticed. What you spend will still be factored into the process and Google always rewards the people who put in the most effort to make their ads more distinct and valuable.

These points are what make AdWords such a valuable service.

Works on More Than Just Google

A great part of Google AdWords is that your ads can show up in places outside Google. You can also use Google's Search Network search partners to make your content visible.

The Google Search Network is a series of search-related sites where your ad can appear, such as YouTube and various other sites that Google operates. You can even get your content to appear on many pages that are outside of Google's reach and have partnered with Google. There is also the option for you to block certain websites on the Search Network.

Additional details on the Search Network will be included later in this guide. The network can be an asset to your marketing needs.

The Display Network is also a point that will be discussed later on. This is a network of sites that Google uses to post many of its ads, but this works differently. In this case, the ads are produced as images or videos. These can appear on any site that Google partners with. YouTube is a good example of this.

A Six-Part Process

This six-part process for AdWords is designed to create a simple approach for managing content.

1. Your AdWords account is free. You will only have to pay for clicks on your ad.

2. The ad campaign is the main campaign that you will use for promoting a certain product or service. You can use as many ad campaigns as you wish. The key is to keep each of these campaigns separate from one another. One product or service will be in one campaign and so forth.

3. Ad groups are attached to each campaign. Your individual campaigns can have many ad groups. These include groups that target different people or other subsections of what you want to highlight in your campaign. Each ad group is separate from each other based on keywords, the content used in each ad and so forth.

4. Keywords must be included in each ad group. The keywords are vital to have people find your ad. These keywords must be related to whatever you are trying to market.

5. Ad text has to be created to establish a visually attractive ad that someone will want to read. Your ad text can include a phrase featuring a keyword you want to target or a marketing ploy you want to use. Whatever

it is, you would have to make it relevant to your ad group.

6. The landing page is the last part. This is where a person will go to after clicking on your link. The landing page should be something on your website that is useful and viable. You must create a smart landing page that is appealing and worth reading.

Setting a Budget

A budget must also be established for your AdWords account. A budget will help you show that you have a plan. Specifically, your budget will show how committed you are to getting your ad exposed.

A budget will specify a certain total for each click that people make on your ads. AdWords is programmed so that you will only have to spend money based on the number of times that people click on your ads.

You will also have the option to post a limit on how much you want to spend on your ads each day. This could be perfect if you want to keep your funds for a campaign in check. There is a chance that your ad might be blocked later in the day because you have gone over your budget for the day.

Chapter 3 – Pros and Cons of Google AdWords

There are many positive aspects of Google AdWords that make it a popular choice for people aiming to make their sites visible online. However, there are some issues that need to be considered.

Pros

Some of the positive aspects of AdWords that make it a popular choice for your marketing:

1. AdWords helps businesses stay more competitive. AdWords is engineered to be about more than just how much money you spend on your advertisements. It is also about how well your ads are designed. You will have to choose the keywords you want to use, the markets you want to target, and how your ad copy is designed.

   You are in a competition – to using the right content, to make your site stand out as you contend with others, and to create the best.

   You will be encouraged to work harder to be more innovative. AdWords focuses on ensuring the landing pages of each AdWords link are accurate. When a site has more unique things or innovations to offer, it becomes easier for AdWords to promote your site.

2. AdWords allows you to use very specific keywords, other bits of ad copy so each ad is unique, and various extensions that you may add. You have full control over your AdWords experience.

The specific nature of AdWords also ensures that you can reach a greater number of people. You can ask to reach specific people based on factors like location, market, and various demographics. AdWords also lets you configure your targets with a simple interface that gives you extra control over your content.

3. You can measure how well your campaign is running. The Analytics features that AdWords uses will give you a clear idea of what is happening with your campaign - to find information on how many people are visiting your site, what you are spending on each click, and which ads are the most effective.

4. Your link will be more visible when you use AdWords. Your link will appear online at the top of a search. The simple design of AdWords ensures that your content will be easy to find.

5. Your budget can be as big or small as you want. With AdWords, you can spend anything you want on your daily budget for each click. You need to decide on a daily, weekly, or monthly budget. If it is not sufficient, your ad could go offline because you reached your budget.

6. It is very easy to produce ads. You just have to get on AdWords and then quickly configure the words you are using or the keywords you want to use. The interface Google provides gives you easy control over your AdWords experience.

You also have the right to produce ads about almost anything. You would still be subjected to some content rules posted by Google about what you can and cannot do with your site, but the rules are easy to follow.

Cons (and How to Resolve Them)

As great as AdWords is, you have to be aware of some of the problems that you could encounter.

1. The competition for AdWords can be great. There are multiple businesses marketing similar things on Google. You might have to spend extra just to get your content to be visible within searches for some of the more popular keywords.

2. Watch for your advertising budget. AdWords has alleviated this issue by allowing you to spread out your daily ad budget over much of the day. However, it only takes a burst of traffic at one time to deplete your daily budget and have your ad removed the rest of the day. The good news is that you can use some parameters when creating your ads for when you want them to show up and how they will appear.

3. There is always a chance that your ads will be targeted to the wrong people. These include people who are not in your target demographics. You might spend money on clicks from people who would not have an interest in what you are offering.

   Google lets you configure your ads to target people in certain geographic areas or people in specific demographics. These configurations help you to keep your content from being shown to the wrong people. You have to monitor the Analytics on your campaign carefully to ensure that you are not spending more money on certain ads than what you can handle.

4. There are limits to your ads. In addition to limits on what types of content you can promote, there are also

limits on how big your ads can be. You can only use 80 characters for the description of an ad, for instance. The character limits are even shorter for other bits of content including extensions. This requires you to be precise and cautious when trying to create ads that stand out.

5. You cannot afford to ignore your landing pages. People who use AdWords often assume that their landing pages aren't a concern. Google values these landing pages and AdWords will analyze the landing pages of its ads and then rank those ads based on how effective the content is. You have to analyze your landing page to see that it flows perfectly and is easy to load. The page must also relate to the content you are trying to promote.

These pros and cons of AdWords deserve to be explored as you look at how well AdWords can be used.

Chapter 4 – Key Parts of a Google AdWords Listing

Enter a keyword on Google. The odds are you will see lots of details on the ads you see on the top. For instance, if you entered in "pizza delivery" as a keyword, the Google AdWords listings that appear on the very top will include several sections. You might notice a box telling you to order delivery online. You may also see a simple tagline.

Every Google AdWords listing is different. An AdWords listing has many parts.

Heading

The heading is the first part of your AdWords listing that users will notice and is a vital part of your marketing. This is the area that the user will click onto. It will lead the user to a site of your choosing, particularly your landing page.

The heading will include the name of your site and keywords relating to what you have to sell. It might include a promotional message or something that piques the user's interest.

URL Listing

The URL listing on your AdWords link is important to its success. You can add small extensions to the end of that URL listing to add an extra description of what you are offering on that listing.

This area on the listing is highlighted in green. It appears right under the heading and is very easy for anyone to notice.

There should be a listing that says "Ad" with a border around it when you make this part of the URL listing. This is used to let the visitor know that the message is an ad. This is a fair display to show that you are directly advertising on Google.

You can adjust the URL in a unique fashion. The main URL of your link will lead people to your side, but you can use a few additional keywords or descriptors next to the URL. You can use this in any way you want if the descriptors are relevant to the URL.

Full Description

The description is the plain text layout that will explain everything about the product you have to offer on your site. It is restricted to a maximum of 80 characters.

You can do all kinds of things with your description. You can add information about what your business does in general, what you have to sell, or any special offers you have. You can also ask a question or tease a product by piquing the user's interest. Some of the keywords you are targeting may be naturally incorporated into the listing, but you would have to keep everything attractive and informative.

Sub-Heads

Sub-heads are placed at the bottom of your advertisement. These are points that will link people to specific sections on your website. You can enter certain sub-heads into your listing and they will appear when Google deems they are relevant to a search. These will direct the user to certain URLs on your site and will add a convenient design that lets people know more about your site.

With sub-heads, people will see that your site is divided into a series of sections. These might include specific points on all the products and services you have to offer. This lets people see how legitimate your site is. This, in turn, makes it easier for you to make your content more attractive and appealing.

Sub-heads are not required when you're trying to get a listing ready. But these are still recommended because they allow people to see your site in a unique fashion. These sub-heads might be a little more descriptive and distinct than anything else you are using at a given time.

Extensions

You have the option to add some extensions to your site to add something appealing to your advertisement. These extensions may work well for letting people know about stuff like a phone number for people to contact you, a link to an app and much more.

Chapter 5 – How to Sign Up and Set Up Payments

To have Google AdWords work for you, you first have to sign up for the service. Fortunately, it is not too hard for you to get this going. You will need to add all the information to your account as accurately and detailed as possible. You must also decide how you will handle your payments.

The Signup Process

1. Go to the official Google AdWords site at adwords.google.com

2. Click on the Start Now icon on the front page.

3. Enter your email address and the website URL.

4. You may be asked questions relating to how you want AdWords to work for you.

   Google will direct you toward different pages depending on what you want to do with your AdWords campaign. You can say that you want to draw people to either your website or a physical location.

   You might also be asked to provide Google with details of the type of campaign you want to use. Let's skip these points for the moment so you can focus on the Google campaign you want to use.

5. Confirm the information relating to your business.

   You will have to confirm your billing country, your time zone, and the currency you will use. Google serves people throughout the world and has a diverse array of currencies to choose from.

6. Check your payments profile.

Your payments should be handled through Google Play. This is a popular payment setup that you will link to a bank account or credit card. You might have noticed this when using the Google Play store on an Android-powered device. The same payment used there will work on AdWords.

You might have to produce a new payments profile if you do not have one already. This should include information about your credit card or bank account. You might have to send proper confirmation stating that you hold the correct account or that you can confirm ownership or a credit card; the rules for this will vary. Be prepared to wait a bit for this to be confirmed.

7. Enter your name and address.

The address should be the place where your business originates. If the business operates from your home, you can enter your home address.

8. Enter your payment setup.

The payment setup should match your payments profile, but you should still confirm that a particular credit or debit card or bank account will be used for the transactions.

The setup should have automatic payments. An automatic charge may happen when you have reached a billing threshold or when 30 days have passed since your last automatic payment.

This process should only take a few moments to complete, although it might take some time depending on any approvals that are needed. You can always change these points on your AdWords account later through the settings menu.

The purpose of this process is to help you do more than just connect to Google AdWords. This also assists you to identify many points that you can use when getting your campaign running. Google can review your location and the campaign you are using to help you decide how to target the right people. Be sure you are as specific as possible when getting your account set up.

Getting Your Balance Ready

You will need to establish an account balance as soon as possible to help you pay for AdWords. There are a few steps you can use to get your account balance prepared:

1. As you get onto your AdWords budget, go to the settings section. Look for the wrench logo.

2. Click on the Billing and Payments section.

3. Click on the Payment Methods section.

4. Review the payment method that you want to use or add a new option.You can use a credit or debit card or a bank account. Google will need to review your content to ensure you can have made the proper deposit.

5. Review the process for how you will pay. When you start using AdWords, you should establish a limit where an automatic debit will occur when your balance reaches a certain total. This threshold might change.

6. You can always go back to this page later to make a payment. For instance, you can make a deposit to

AdWords to pay for a part of your account balance before you get to the threshold or the end of a 30-day billing period.

Be sure to arrange a proper payment solution, which will have to be an automatic payment in order to use AdWords. You will be at risk of being banned from AdWords altogether if you are unable to pay what is owing on time.

Understanding Your Billing Threshold

When you sign up for AdWords, you will notice that you can only spend a certain amount of money on your ads each month. The threshold is a limit to ensure that you only spend a determined amount that you know you can afford. You might have to increase this amount as you start to use AdWords more often and have a larger budget for your ads.

Your billing threshold will be set at $50 at the beginning. Over time, your threshold will expand based on how often people are clicking on your site. You might get a billing threshold of $200 after some time. This will then increase to $350 and later to $500.

Make sure you are spending enough money on your campaign at this juncture. Your threshold will only increase after you have spent a certain amount within a 30-day period. Therefore, if you only spent $10 in a month, your threshold will stay at $50. You would have to get to the $50 mark for you to go to the next level.

Don't forget that you will be automatically billed once you reach that threshold. Be sure that your card or bank account has enough money for you to handle the billing period when it comes around. Remember that you can still make manual payments before you get to that threshold or the end of your 30-day period.

Tax Exemption Points

Note: This next section is for people in the United States. Contact Google for more information on taxes relating to how AdWords works if you are from outside the United States.

Your business might be able to claim a tax exemption for using Google AdWords. You will likely be able to claim business income from the ads you are posting. To do so, you would have to include Google and its Tax Identification Number of 77-0493581 as a part of your business taxes. However, you can apply for a tax exemption. Getting your tax exemption is easy when you list Google LLC as the seller. Google is giving you extra help to have sales handled:

1. Go to the Billing and Payments section of your site.

2. Click on the Settings section.

3. Go to the Tax Exemption Info section of the page.

4. Enter your tax exemption number.

5. The start and end dates of your tax exemption can be entered if you know them. This is an optional feature.

6. You can also include details on the exemption type if you have it, but this is also optional.

7. A file including your exemption details must be included. Google LLC must be listed as the seller.

8. Later, check back to review the status of your tax exemption.

It might take some time to have the tax exemption reviewed. Google will let you know when the listing has been accepted.

Chapter 6 – Adjusting Access Levels

After you have signed up for Google AdWords, you will have the option to allow other people in your business to access the account. This is valuable because getting people to work on your site makes it easier for many campaigns that you might want to use.

You will need these access levels to ensure that you have more control over your campaign. You will need people in your workplace to assist you with getting your content up and running and accessible.

There are four access levels that you can use. Be sure these are provided to the right people based on their capabilities and how responsible you feel these people are:

1. Admin - is the person who receives notifications and reports and can sign in to review reports. The Admin can also accept or refuse account link requests.

   The Admin has more power than anyone else on AdWords. You should be designated the Admin. As the Admin, you will have the final say. You have the option to consider letting another person be the Admin, but that person should be an assistant or someone else in your workplace who fully understands what you are doing with your project.

2. Standard - is the level of access allows a person to receive notification emails and reports while also having the ability to control many reports. Standard users do not have as many controls as the Admin, but it can be useful for those who are trained in using AdWords.

Your standard access workers will help you produce quality content while reviewing what you are going to produce. The general goal is to create enough content that is appealing and worthwhile.

3. Read-Only - this level allows people to read details on your campaigns in real time. Those people cannot actually control the platform or adjust anything.

   You can use the Read-Only access level for people who can help you with creating ads and other messages without actually giving those people full access.

4. Email-Only - this level is for people to receive information on what you are doing through emails. This does not entail real-time reviews of what is happening.

   You will have to carefully choose the particular account levels that you want to give to people. The people who are most likely to be responsible for your account and the data should be given the appropriate access.

Adjusting the Levels of Access Yourself

You will need to look at these roles when getting your page and your campaign ready. Consider who in your workplace is appropriate to assign certain tasks.

You should only offer access to people who clearly understand what you want to do with your AdWords efforts. Make sure those people are comfortable with what you are doing and that you are providing them with a sensible amount of information on what can be done in a situation and how a campaign can be run in some form.

The steps for adjusting access levels are as follows:

1. Click on the Settings menu on your AdWords page. The Settings menu is represented by a wrench icon.

2. Go to the Account Access section.

3. Click on the Plus sign.

4. Enter the email address of a person you want to access followed by the specific access level that you want to give to that person.

5. You will then send an invitation to the person you are giving access.

When that person agrees to the invitation, he or she will be added to your access list. That person will have access to the benefits that come with the particular access level.

Adjusting the access levels might not sound like something important, but there's a reason why it is vital. You will have to allow many people in your workplace to have access to provide you with extra help.

Chapter 7 – Linking Accounts

The next thing you need to do is to set up your AdWords account with any linked accounts you might have. Linking your accounts is a simple and easy to follow.

You can use AdWords with many other websites and services operated by Google. These include:

- <u>Google Analytics</u> provides you with information on website metrics, conversion data and much more.

- <u>Google Firebase</u> works for app installs and actions. You can link Firebase up to AdWords to track actions where people might download the apps you have to offer.

- <u>Google Play</u> tracks information on people who download your app. This lets you adjust your marketing campaign.

- <u>Salesforce</u> will show you how to trigger offline conversions. Linking your account with Salesforce helps you to identify sales data while linking it to your AdWords page.

- <u>YouTube</u> can give you information on actions people take when they interact with any ads you post on YouTube.

- <u>Merchant Center</u> account can be used if you are going to run a shopping campaign.

To work with linked accounts:

1. Go to the settings section of your AdWords account. Look for the wrench icon.

2. Select the Linked Accounts option.

3. Review the individual account pages that you can use.

4. Click the Details button on any of the accounts that you want to link. After reviewing the content, click on the Link button.

5. Follow the appropriate instructions.

The instructions that you will need to follow will vary with each option. For example:

- For Google Analytics, you must check your Analytics account and get Google Optimize to work.

- For Firebase, you must create an account and then set it up with your AdWords account.

- YouTube integration works when you either own a channel yourself or you get permission from someone who owns a channel.

- Other programs might require you to enter the email address for whoever owns an account that you want to link. The account owner will have to approve the request to get the content linked to AdWords. This clearly works best if you own the account that you want to link yourself.

If someone else owns an account that you are linking to, that person will not have the ability to adjust your AdWords account. You will not be able to control that other person's account, so you will have to get that person to help you with configuring things on your setup to make your link work.

Linking Third-Party Apps for Mobile Use

You can use various third-party apps with AdWords. There are far too many apps to discuss here, but you can use a few steps for getting one of these apps supported on your AdWords account:

1. Go to the Third-Party App Analytics option on the Linked Accounts section.

2. Click the Create Link ID option.

3. Select the platform that you are working with. This is either the Android or iOS option.

4. Enter the name of the app that you wish to use. Select the option that you wish to use in this case.

You have the option to automatically choose one of many more popular Analytics apps like AppsFlyer, Singular, TUNE, Adways, and Kochava among others. Many of these programs focus on certain tracking programs, but the functionality for each program could work differently for your needs when marketing your content.

Check the instructions for each app you can use to get an idea of what to expect out of your content.

You will learn more about working with many linked accounts throughout this guide. No matter what you use, you must look at how well your accounts are managed and that you plan everything accordingly.

Chapter 8 – Choosing Keywords

Now that you are on AdWords, you have to begin by choosing the appropriate keywords that you want to use. These are the magic words that will make your online marketing efforts be successful. Using them correctly is a vital part of running a campaign.

You have to use only the best possible keywords to provide you with a chance to make your campaign visible.

You will have to go online to find keywords and this will require a lot of effort.

You should also know that there is an extensive number of keywords for you to work with and the competition has to be considered.

Choosing Your Keywords

Every business has its own series of keywords that it will use. How can you tell which keywords are the right ones to use?

The answer is simple – you're going to have to decide this yourself. You can get a better idea if you just look around your site and get a clear idea of everything you want to do with your marketing efforts.

You can use these steps to choose keywords.

1. Review each page on your website.

    Take a look at the copy on your website. See what words are used often and how they might be unique. You might find some keywords that are more relevant and useful than others.

    Write down whatever words or phrases you notice on your pages that are more consistent or noteworthy than others. You should find enough of these throughout your entire page.

For this example, let's say that you run a women's fashion store. You might have various phrases on your website relating to contemporary or modern fashions. You could start by using keywords like "modern women's fashion" or "contemporary women's style". These are relatively broad in that you're just talking about women's clothing. Think of other unique descriptive words that could describe your business.

2. Consider the needs that your customers have.

Look at what your customers might be thinking when they visit your website. What types of things might they want to find? What do you think they would type into a Google search when trying to find your page? Look at what people might consider and see that your keywords relate to whatever it is they might have the most interest in finding.

The needs that people have for your site will vary. For women's clothes, you might hear stories about new trends in fashion or popular types of clothes that women need at a very specific time of the year. "Women's swimwear" would surely do better in the spring or summer than "women's coats," a keyword that you should focus on during the fall and winter seasons.

3. Identify the demographics of your customers.

The demographics that you reach can be adjusted later through AdWords, but you should think about those demographics sooner. You can always review points on the prospective audience that you might target. This helps you to see what specific keywords you have to use.

While "women's swimwear" might be a good keyword, you could choose something more specific. Are you trying to target younger women? Maybe a keyword like "young women's swimwear" or "juniors swimwear" might be better. Perhaps you are looking to target people who are smaller in size. Something like "petite swimwear" can be used in this case.

Maybe people have specific interests. Women who are more athletic might look for a keyword like "athletic swimwear." You have to use various types of keywords based on the demographics of the people you are targeting. This narrows your focus, but it also brings you closer to the people who are more likely to use your site.

4. Start working with the broadest keywords.

When you come up with your keywords, you have to start by using some keywords that cover more bases. These broad keywords are not specific but will be the key to creating more creative search words.

You can start by thinking about the basics. When talking about women's shirts, you might start with keywords like "women's tops" or "women's shirts." Eventually, you can move toward more specific keywords like "women's long-sleeve shirts" or "women's hooded shirts" among other choices.

5. Start being more specific.

   The "women's shirts" keyword might become "women's green shirts" or "women's plus-size shirts" among other things. You may also refer to specific sizes or other extremely distinct features. Keywords like "women's 2x shirts" or "women's medium size shirts" might work. The key is to think about something extremely specific or distinct that would not be considered by too many of your competitors. Something that focuses on a very particular product you have is always worth adding.

6. Create new variations for those specific keywords.

   Find as many variations of the keywords as you can. These variants should include several choices that cover many points relating to certain outfits. The keyword "women's green shirts" can branch out into many more distinct keywords like "women's green tees," "green shirts for women," "women's green t-shirts" or "women's green tops."

   The key is to think about as many synonyms as possible for the words you are choosing. The word "shirt" has many synonyms. By using as many as you can, you will cover more angles in terms that people might use to search. Don't forget to include abbreviations into your work and even plural forms. Things like "Ts," "shirts" and "tee" are all good options.

7. Start working with long-tail keywords that are specific.

   Long-tail keywords are keywords that are longer in length and have more identifying factors. It might not get as many search results as other keywords, but it will do more for you when people actually search for your store based on those keywords. A person who enters in a long-tail keyword will have a very specific need. By using such keywords, you will target people who have those particular needs, thus giving you a better chance at getting people to pay attention to whatever you have to offer.

A good example of a long-tail keyword would be "women's green sleeveless shirt." This is not going to be as popular as "women's green shirt" or "green sleeveless shirt," but you are adding that extra modifier into the keyword. This makes it easier for people to notice your content and see that you are talking about a very specific type of product.

Also, you should spend less on these long-tail keywords than what you might spend elsewhere. The problem with many smaller keywords is that they are far too competitive. You would surely have to spend more on one of these keywords just to be noticed. With a long-tail one, the competition involved will be much smaller. This means you can reduce the amount of money you would spend on your searches when you have enough long-tail keywords to work with.

8. Decide how the keywords will be laid out based on the content you are sharing.

The keywords you are producing need to be organized based on how they will appear. You must see how the keywords are going to look based on whether they are sensible or easy to follow.

The problem with some keywords is that they might be very difficult to naturally incorporate into your content. You have to produce keywords that are easy to follow and are not complicated. Everything must appear sensible or else your descriptions will be difficult to read and therefore less effective.

AdWords will review how your landing pages are related to your keywords. Your ads will not be likely to show up if AdWords deems that your content is not relevant to the keywords you want to highlight. Be ready to adjust your site if you need to keep certain keywords. Better yet, try to just change those keywords from the start if only to make it easier for the content to look appropriate.

The Four Main Types of Keywords

There are four types of keywords. You should plan your marketing campaign based on the certain keywords that you want to highlight. This is to create a better layout for making your content stand out.

1. Brand - a word that includes the name of a brand or trademark.

   Let's say that a sportswear and sports equipment store was developing a PPC campaign. Maybe it might want to tell people that it offers various products from the Adidas Company. The store would use various brand keywords that include that brand name in it. These include keywords like "Adidas shoes," "Adidas shirts" or "Adidas shop."

   Using brand keywords might end up being expensive. Sometimes the actual brand itself might be spending the most money to be visible. In this example, the Adidas Company might be spending more money on its own brand keywords than anyone else. The added traffic that gets onto Adidas' website, combined with the devoted focus that site has on its own products, might make it very difficult for people to try and bid on brand keywords without spending massive amounts of money. At best, a person might have the second-highest listing on a search behind the company itself.

You might also be subjected to legal rules surrounding the use of a branded keyword. The brand keyword has to be approved by Google and this might take some time.

2. Competitor - includes the brand names of competitors that are directly in competition with someone. These include those who are in the same field and offer identical products or services.

The sportswear store would use keywords that include the names of the companies Adidas is directly competing with to draw attention to itself. This may work to cover all of the store's bases. Keywords like "Nike shoes," "Fila shoes" or "Under Armour apparel" might work in this case.

Anyone who uses competitor keywords must do so with caution. Such keywords might be misleading. You would not want to go to a site that sells Adidas apparel if you are looking for Nike apparel, for instance.

Competitor keywords are often more expensive to work with as you are still using the same keywords that have direct brand names in them. You would want to watch carefully for who is spending the most on these keywords as the brands themselves might be spending all that money. Besides, those brands are probably capable of actually spending that amount money because they can afford to do so.

Again, be aware that the approval for using a keyword may take some time. You might have to wait a few days before you can get approved to use a keyword that features a brand name even if you are competing with it.

3. Generic - a term that relates to certain types of products or services without including any brand names. Our sporting goods store would use generic terms like "running shoes," "basketball shorts" or "training wear." Sometimes those terms might be a little more specific but still retain their generic appeal. Words like "boys basketball shorts" or "girls athletic wear" or "plus-size athletic apparel" might be used when trying to attract certain groups of people.

   You can use more words or terms in your generic keywords. By adding more words, you can create something more specific or at least be able to reach more people based on the content being offered.

4. Related - a term that does not necessarily relate to what a site is selling. Instead, the term includes information on something that people might be searching for at a given time.

   A related term may include something involving the actions that people might engage in while using the products sold by a company. A sports equipment store will include terms like "jogging," "basketball" or "baseball." Anything that is more specific like "baseball practice" or "soccer lessons" might be better.

Try to stay within your genre or field of work if possible. Don't choose keywords that do not have a real relation to anything you are offering. Your listing could be penalized if your keywords have nothing to do with your subject matter or the field of work that you are trying to promote.

Always Use Relevant Keywords

No matter what you planning to do, you must ensure that the keywords you have are relevant to your website. You should not use keywords that have no real meaning to your site or else you might not get the results that you want.

When you're trying to market sports equipment, you have to use keywords that relate to sports, sporting goods, and even the brand names of companies that sell those products. You could even use keywords like "basketball practice," "baseball training" or "tennis accessories" if you want. The key is to see that the keywords are relevant in some way so that a person on your site might have a need to use the products you sell.

AdWords might penalize your listing if you have keywords that mean nothing to your content. Also, these unrelated keywords might be problematic because they bring people who have no interest in your product. This, in turn, would keep you from spending your budget on the people who would actually have an interest in your product.

Using Misspelled Words

Have you tried to enter some word into a search engine but you weren't fully certain as to how it was spelled? It is completely understandable as some words might be a challenge to spell. You can cover more bases by intentionally targeting misspelled words.

Let's look at a different example for a moment. A retailer might be trying to sell kosher food products for people in the

Jewish community. That group might be looking to sell grape juice from Manischewitz, one of the most popular names in the field of kosher foods. That brand name is very difficult for some people to spell.

Therefore, the retailer would start to target people with misspelled keywords. A person might know how to say the name but not necessarily how to spell it. Targeting people with such misspelled words might help to reach more them. For instance, the keyword "Manischewitz grape juice" can be paired with other keywords like "Manichewitz grape juice," "Menichawitz grape juice" or anything else that might sound the same but is spelled differently. A keyword like "Manischewitz grape juice" could also be used for people who might accidentally misspell a much easier word.

You will be impressed at how using such misspellings might target people who have a certain intention but haven't been able to reach your site for whatever reason. Besides, many of these misspellings are ones that people often forget about. They never think about them until they notice that their searches have something that says "did you mean..."

Consider Voice Searches

Some of the most popular searches on Google aren't only searches people enter through a keyboard. People are also searching for things by talking into their mobile devices. Here's an example.

1. A person is trying to find information on where she can find jogging apparel for herself.

2. They would open up her mobile device and say, "Where can I find jogging clothes?" or "Who sells jogging outfits for women?"

3. They would then get a page that shows the results of retailers in her area or retailers online that offer jogging apparel.

This is a special form of technology that makes it easier for people to find things online. It is also something that should influence how you work with particular keywords. You would have to come up with keywords that sound like ones that people say.

Look at the keywords that you have come across. Do any of them sound like things people would incorporate into a question that they might ask? If so, then you are on the right track as you are working with keywords that people would have a vested interest in. If not, you should adjust your plans and find new keywords that people might realistically use. Doing so improves your chances to succeed.

Think about different types of questions that people could ask. Starters like "Where can I," "How can I, "Who sells," or "Where is" can be considered. Using enough of these keywords will help you to grow your keyword listing while working with your content.

This might also work with Google Home devices. You could use a keyword relating to some localized product. When a person says "Who can I order pizza from," Google Home would verbally list information on a nearby pizza place. You could use that "Who can I order pizza from" keyword when making your content attractive and easy to find.

Using Negative Keywords

Negative keywords are the keywords that you do not want your site to appear in search results. This is vital for helping you to control your expenses. The problem with having your site show up because of unwanted keywords is that you might spend more on your campaign than necessary. This is due to either people clicking on a link by mistake or maybe by your link getting too many impressions depending on the type of campaign you follow.

Sometimes certain modifiers of your keywords might be irrelevant and potentially insulting to your client base. What if you were selling high-end vacuum cleaners with lots of features? These cleaners might cost extra for people to but, but they will be more effective in their work than what you might get from some other place. You would have to include keywords relating to words like "cheap" or "discount" as negative keywords as those are clearly not things that people would consider when finding high-quality cleaners that might cost a little extra and are not as likely to appear on discount sites.

You can use these steps for having negative keywords work for you:

1. Check your search reports based on what your site takes in.

   Look at any search reports you can get regarding your site. See how people might have found your page based on certain keyword searches. Maybe some of them are getting there through keywords that you don't want to use. You can figure out the most problematic keywords in this situation by looking to see what is being used at a given time.

2. Determine the types of words in your negative keywords that are not relevant to your product.

   You clearly would want to avoid using keyword types like "free" if you are not going to give away anything.

3. As you develop your negative keyword listing, you can add the modifiers to the words you have.

   In this case, you can use the word "free" over your regular keywords and include them as negative keywords. This ensures that the keyword you are using will never show up on any search where someone might be looking for free things.

4. Avoid using too many negative keywords.

   It is perfectly fine to use negative keywords, but you must watch how you get them to work for you. Do not use lots of negative keywords or else it might be a challenge for you to get your site to become visible.

Expand Your Keywords by Using Several Parameters

Expand on your keyword list by using many parameters within those words. Your keywords can include an extensive variety of identifying points.

For instance, your sporting goods store might need to use keywords to identify many factors. You might want to focus on things like the type of product you want to sell, the activity it may be useful for and so forth. You can grow your keyword list with these steps:

1. Determine at least three types of words that you might use in a keyword.

   For instance, when coming up with sports-related keywords, you might use – the sport involved, the type of product to sell, and any identifying point relating to that product.

You can use many synonyms for those words. The goal is to have enough of these words to create distinct keywords that people might use in their searches.

2. Start thinking in terms of the first type of word.

   Look at terms for the sports your site might be involved with promoting. Words relating to baseball, volleyball, field hockey, ice hockey, tennis or jogging could be used. You must use keywords that are relevant to your site. A site that doesn't offer football items might not want to use that term, for instance.

3. Choose the second word.

   The second word should be something that identifies the specific product you are selling. It could have words relating to size, the type of person that would use it, and the color of the product and so forth.

4. The last type of word should be the specific product or service you have to offer. Use as many variations of that word as possible.

   For sports apparel and equipment, you can use many words relating to the specific products you sell. You can list details of shoes, shorts, shirts, balls, sticks, nets and anything else you have to market.

5. Combine the three words together into as many reasonable combinations as possible.

   The emphasis here is to be reasonable. You can combine the word "basketball" from the first column with "men's" from the second and "shoes" from the third to create "men's basketball shoes." This is a sensible layout that someone might surely look for.

The best part of this process is that you can use it to create a huge variety of keywords. Always make sure the words are sensible and that they relate to things that you actually have for sale on your website.

Managing Long-Tail Keywords

Long-tail keywords will let you target specific groups while potentially spending less money on your efforts, but you must also look at how well these keywords are designed.

Long-tail keywords will require you to add more content and use many extra words. These include special descriptors that add something valuable to your content. There are many things you can do to create long-tail keywords:

1. Use the Keyword Planner tool to find information on which keywords are being used and by which people.

   This tool, which will be covered in a later chapter, will give you information on how certain keywords are being used at any given time. This includes details on how many people are searching for things based on those keywords in question.

2. Use as many adjectives relating to your products as you can.

   Using just one adjective per keyword phrase is good enough. But you should at least have enough of these adjectives to create several keywords combinations. When talking about vacuum cleaners, you could use adjectives like "self-propelled," "automatic," "fast" or "eco-friendly". This adds new long-tail keywords that explain more about what you have to offer. Choose many adjectives as long as they all relate to what you are offering.

3. See how the adjectives relate to your Unique Selling Proposition or USP.

   The adjectives must be relevant and they directly relate to what you have to offer. You should only use "eco-friendly vacuum cleaners" as a long-tail keyword if you do have vacuum cleaners that use less energy and don't require chemical cleaners.

4. Look at Google's autocomplete feature.

   Sometimes you might find some great long-tail keywords just by using the autocomplete feature on Google's main site. Just enter "vacuum cleaner" and you will see many options like "vacuum cleaner parts," "vacuum cleaner bags," "vacuum cleaner hospital" and much more. These give you good ideas for what to use; you might say that a vacuum cleaner you sell is appealing to have in a hospital where air quality is at a premium.

   The things you will see on the autocomplete feature are all relatively broad. By entering "vacuum cleaner hospital", you might notice several local areas in the search box. You might see things like "vacuum cleaner hospital Shreveport." That keyword would clearly target hospitals and health professionals in the Shreveport area who might need quality vacuum cleaners for their use, but this would still be a worthwhile endeavor to consider.

5. Check out the related keywords on the bottom of a Google search.

   After you enter a keyword into Google, you can find possible long-tail keywords at the bottom of a page. When you look for vacuum cleaners, you might find long-tail keywords like "vacuum cleaners for sale," "vacuum cleaner brands" or "vacuum cleaner stick" among other things.

   There are no rules for how many long-tail keywords you can use. Try to add as many of them as you can. You will still keep the same daily budget. You will just have more keywords to make it potentially easier for people to find your content.

Use Your Keywords Naturally

There is one final point to consider when making a list of keywords. You have to only use keywords that you know sound natural and genuine. These include keywords that are going to blend in well with the content on your site.

The keywords should fit in well with your ad and your website without making it harder for you to see what's on an ad. Some ads are problematic because they have keywords added at random. A user might stop reading in order to figure out the context.

Chapter 9 – Keyword Matches

Now that you have your keywords, you can start thinking about how you are going to make them work. To get this to run to your benefit, you have to look at how Google will identify your keywords.

As you enter keywords into Google, you will see that your content will reveal many results. Sometimes you might get the exact things that you want. In other cases, you will get results that might be very different from what you expected, especially on the second or third pages of results.

You will have to look at how your keywords match up while using AdWords. Keyword matches are points where you are letting Google know that you want your keyword to show up in some form. You can use this to be a little broader in what you are willing to share. The four types of keyword matches you can use are the following (ranging from the most restrictive to the least):

1. **Exact Match**

   The exact match option is extremely restrictive. Google will only place your ads on queries that are the exact keyword or phrase that you are linking to.

   You might be using a keyword like "basketball shorts." The exact match option will list your query only on searches that use the words "basketball shorts" exactly as they appear. No words will appear before or after that phrase. Although this provides you with a direct focus on a specific keyword, you would also be less likely to get people to see that listing because of how limited it is in reach.

The exact match results are always the first ones that come up. These are the most relevant to your site or ad. These might also be very expensive for you to target due to how specific the search might be.

2. Phrase Match

A phrase match involves your keyword is displayed only when a full phrase is involved. The "basketball shorts" example can work with keyword searches like "where can I buy basketball shorts" or "black and white basketball shorts" or "basketball shorts for women" among other things.

This is a little more flexible and works well with spoken queries. It is also good for when you're trying to target people who type in questions. However, the words in your phrase match must appear in the proper order. Naturally, anything more specific like "red basketball shorts" would be restrictive as you'd have to get someone to type in something like "red basketball shorts for sale" or "who sells red basketball shorts near me" in order to make your ad show up.

Phrase matches actually do well for spoken word searches. This makes it essential for you to target speech-related search keywords, especially when you're trying to reach people through mobile devices or to make your business easier for Google Home to announce.

3. Modified Broad Match

A modified broad match is when your result shows up only when a search has the full phrase. You might use a search word like "basketball shorts," but this would work only when it matches the words of your phrase. A search that uses the keyword "basketball shorts for sale" or "orange basketball shorts" would target your site.

4. **Broad Match**

The broad match is the least restrictive option to work with. It is also the default option you will use. At this point, your keyword will link to various types of searches no matter what they might be. For instance, your basketball shorts site might link up to a search like "shorts for basketball" or "basketball apparel" or "athletic shorts." It could even appear in searches for related words like "sports outfits."

Plan as many of these keywords as you can for each category. Using more of them gives you a great plan for making your keywords dynamic and effective.

Which Option Works Best?

A broad match is useful for when you are trying to use keywords that have broad meanings themselves. An exact match is better if you are trying to target an extremely specific audience with your products or services.

For instance, you might try to sell big and tall outfits, but a broad match would not work well in that case. People might find your site when looking for clothing products in general. These include people who don't need big and tall apparel. They will have wasted their time on your site while you will have spent money on a click from someone who did not need your site to begin with.

You could avoid this problem by using an exact match instead of a broad match. You would not have as many people see your ad, but the ones that are looking for big and tall apparel will at least find it.

A phrase match might also do well if you are trying to highlight outfits in general. This would add a bit of flexibility provided that you are specifically talking about having big and tall apparel.

The general rule of thumb is to think about how specific you want to be when trying to market your product. A broad match is good if you are trying to concentrate on general products, but an exact match might be better if you are trying to target people based on a very specific content.

You can always use multiple types of keywords based on the matches you use. Mixing phrase and exact keywords can add a better layout where you are covering more of your bases. You have the final choice as to what you would get out of the process.

Chapter 10 – Setting Up Ad Groups

You will need to design your campaign after you have set up the keywords that you want to work with. At this point, you will have to consider how to work with ad groups.

An ad group is a grouping of keywords that you will use in that campaign. By using the right ad groups with the best content in each one, you will have an easier time with getting your campaign to run well.

You can use as many ad groups as you want. You can get them all organized with an appropriate amount of content and data based on what you want to offer to people with your promotions. To make an ad group work, you have to have a clear idea of what to expect out of an ad group.

Understanding the Concept

To get an ad group to work for you, it helps to first understand what makes an ad group valuable. An ad group is a container that you will use for the keywords you are targeting within a campaign.

The ad groups can all be different from one another within your ad campaign. These groups include three points:

1. **Keywords**

   First, you will put the keywords into an ad group. These are the words that your search will be directly linked to. You can use as many keywords as you want in your ad group. In fact, you can create different ad groups that focus on various types of keywords. This is perfect if you have a retail site that includes multiple types of products or services.

2. Text Ads

The text ads you create will link to the keywords you are using to associate to a search. Each group needs to have its own text ad. You could have one ad talking about a particular product or service you have to offer and then another ad highlighting something you have to offer.

3. Landing Page

The landing page is the place that a person will access by clicking on your AdWords post. The page will make an impact on how your ad looks. By using a great landing page, you will highlight your work to a great variety of people.

Each ad group can include its own landing page. Sometimes the landing page might be the main home page of your site. In another case, it could lead to a certain section of that site outside of the main page. Your landing page must have a good layout where the content is easy to read and use. It should not be overly complicated.

The landing page must be relevant to the keywords and content you are using. AdWords does take a look at how well your landing page is organized. If AdWords finds that your content is not appropriate, you could be penalized and not get your ads listed properly.

Creating an Ad Group

Google makes it easy for you to do anything you want with your ad group. But as you plan out your ad group, you will have to look at what you will get out of your content. There are three vital points to create an ad group that you must use if you want to make the most out of your work:

1. Everything in your campaign has to be integrated appropriately.

   All the keywords, text ads and landing pages you use in your ad groups have to link up to each other quite well. You can get the keywords to appear in your text ad and landing page if desired. You can also use many sections listed on your landing page on your ad group messages if desired. Making sure all the content is organized well is vital to keeping your content accessible and useful.

   Everything must also appear to be natural. Using fragmented sentences or stuffing into keywords into your ads might not work well. People will only click on your ads if they notice that the content in your ad group is organized right and with a nice design.

2. All the points in your ad group must be consistent.

   Your plans for an ad group must entail the message being consistent and regular all the way through. The message needs a good layout where the content is attractive and easy to follow as the keywords mean the same thing at all times. Anything that keeps the content from being meaningful is always going to hurt.

   The message should be the same all the way through. Each ad group only needs just one particular message for it to work right.

3. Each ad group should also be distinct from one another.

Working with different groups that include various advertisements is always a plus. You can use many ad groups with specific targets or goals added to them. You would have to name these separately from one another to tell them apart. Also, you would have to watch for how individual keywords and extensions are used in each of these ad groups. You will need to lay this content out appropriately to make the most of your work.

Your ad groups are a necessity to review when getting AdWords to work out right. As you will read throughout this guide, each part of your AdWords campaign will go well into getting the most out of your content and making it attractive and easy for people to use and search all around.

How to Create An Ad Group

The process associated with creating your group varies based on the type of campaign you are working with.

1. After entering the campaign you want to add an ad group into, select the Ad Groups option. This will be found on the left-hand side of your menu.

2. Enter a name for the ad group. Make the name as distinct as possible. You can name this after the keywords you are trying to target, or the type of content your ad group includes.

3. Enter details on the keywords you are using within that ad group.

4. At this point, you can create individual ads that link to your ad group. You can use as many of these ads in your group as you want.

5. You may also be given the option to add extensions to your ad group, although the options will vary based on where you go.

The process for creating the ad group will help you make use of new advertisements. Look at how well the content is organized and that you have a great plan for making your ad groups look appealing.

Chapter 11 – Types of Campaigns and Their Goals

You should have an idea of keywords that you want to use in your campaign at this point, but what type of campaign are you going to utilize? How will you get people to see what you are offering while using ads that are appealing and easy to follow? That is what this chapter will explain.

You will have to decide on the particular campaign that you want to use when getting AdWords to work for you. Google offers a variety of campaign options for you. They all operate with different solutions.

A campaign is a set of ad groups that you will use. Your ad groups will blend in with a singular budget and target location. With a campaign, you will organize many of the keywords and other points that you want to use when marketing your business to others. By working with a quality campaign, it will become easier for your business to grow and thrive.

Specific Types of Campaigns

You will have the option to select the type of campaign you wish to run when you are establishing a new project. This is only a brief explanation of what you will encounter when working on a campaign. You can refer to later chapters in this guide for details on how to work with particular solutions. However, it is the first choice that is the most popular.

1. **Search**

   This is the most commonly used type of advertisement that people use with AdWords. It is a basic choice that is not hard to follow and very easy to spot online.

A Search campaign is simply posting a traditional text ad that can be found on a search. This targets people based on the keyword being used and your location. This may also work with many ad extensions including details on a URL, phone number, social media link, and other items that you can add. These details can be added as you plan your listing.

Much of this book focuses on the search campaign solution. It is a basic option that does not require too much effort provided you know how to make this choice work to market on Google.

2. Display

A Display campaign offers a solution for running many types of ads online. You can work with not only a basic search campaign but also post images or videos.

When visiting a third-party website, you will notice lots of advertisements for products or services for other sites. Many of these ads are produced by Google.

You can get your ads to appear on one of more than two million different websites. You can also adjust your display ads to target very specific websites or people. There is also the option to omit certain websites from the program. You will learn more about the Display campaign option later in this guide.

3. Shopping

A Shopping campaign is where you will produce an advertisement that shows up on the top of a page that highlights a product you want to sell. It can have your company's name, the name of a product, its price, and a picture of what you are selling.

This is an intriguing choice that lets people see that you are directly trying to sell a product that someone is searching for.

Your ad may also include a Showcase layout. This is a type of ad where your content will be highlighted with its own special section. This includes a listing of many products on your site paired together within the same listing. For the best results, the layout would require a detailed listing of all the products you have for sale in a certain department.

4. Video

This AdWords campaign focuses on YouTube advertisements. It is similar to what you would see on a standard Google search, but the big difference is that you are getting your advertisement posted on YouTube. This offers an exciting way for you to reach people with your own special video. This can be a fun way to market your work, but you would have to make that video appealing and useful to others.

With a video advertisement, you can get your content to be visible to more people. You need to plan your video ad carefully to show what you have to offer in an interesting way.

5. Universal App

The Universal App program is when you have a mobile app that you want people to install. You can get your ad to appear in the Google Play store and on YouTube's mobile app.

This is an advertising option that requires you to give an explanation to promote an Android or iOS app. Google uses different processes for these two as Android is closely linked with Google. Also, you would have to provide information on your app once it has been published on the Google Play store.

6. **Express**

The Express option is a choice that creates automated advertisements on Google and various other sites that partner with AdWords. This allows for search and display ads.

You can program the Express option based on three different choices. You can use it to either get people to call your business, to get them to visit your storefront, or to take a certain action on your website.

Individual Goals of Each Campaign

When you select the specific campaign you want to use, you will be given the choice as to what goal you want to use. There are many goals for each campaign. Google lets you select a goal that you want to follow and will help you adjust the settings of your campaign based on the goal you select. You have the option to change those settings later; Google just lists these settings as recommendations for what you can do to make your campaign stand out.

Your experience will be different based on the specific content you are using and the goal that you want to reach.

Some of these goals include the following:

1. Sales

You can create a campaign with sales in mind. This helps you to encourage people to take an action like getting app downloads, phone calls, or website visits. With this objective, you will have your AdWords experience adjusted to show that you are interested in getting as many sales as possible when you work on your Google campaign.

This is the most popular goal that people have in mind when planning their AdWords campaign. A sales goal might be having people simply visiting a site to buy products. Some people might spend extra on their bids in this case because they simply know they will get more people to visit their site.

2. Leads

When you aim to get leads, you are building upon your audience potential. You are trying to get people to simply learn more about your business so they will likely click on your page later or visit your physical location.

Leads concentrate more on just getting people to visit a site. This is perfect if you have large-value services or products that you want to sell. For instance, a car dealer could use this goal to inform the public that it has vehicles available for sale.

3. Web Traffic

You can aim to get more web traffic onto your site through this option. Google can tailor your AdWords experience to focus mainly on trying to make your content appealing so people will want to click on a link to your site. This could work if you are trying to get more people to your site even if they are not going to shop there. Besides, sometimes getting more traffic can help you to get your page to become more popular on a search, especially if your site is new and you just want people to know about what you have to offer.

4. **Product and Brand Consideration**

This option is more of an inspirational one. That is, people will be inspired to take a look at your brand or product. You can use this to create visual ads that are more than just text. This is clearly made with display ads in mind.

5. **Brand Awareness**

The Brand Awareness choice focuses on producing attractive image ads while increasing awareness in certain people. These include people who you feel might be more likely to support your brand or at least have some vested interest in it.

These options can help, but you don't necessarily have to choose any of them. Google gives you the option to process without your campaign without having any goals attached to your work. Again, you can always change the objective of your campaign later if you wish.

Do not feel overwhelmed or daunted when you begin to get your campaign started. The different options you have to choose from are vast, but they are all there from Google to help you get your campaign started. Working to produce appealing ads can help you get the most out of AdWords no matter which option you choose.

Chapter 12 – Starting a Campaign

After you have a list of the keywords you want to use, you can get your campaign started. The keywords can go well into your campaign, but you will have to use a few simple steps.

These steps are essentially the same for each campaign no matter what the goal might be. The process described here is for working with a Search campaign.

1. Go to the Campaigns section of your AdWords page.

2. Click on the New Campaign option.

3. Select the type of campaign you want to work with. For this exercise, you will work with a basic Search campaign. This is the most popular and the most basic option.

4. Type in a name for the new campaign.

5. Select the network that you are going to get your campaign to run on. The Search Network is the basic one that you should choose in the beginning. This will create the basic text ad. You can also choose to work with different search partners.

6. Select the location or locations that you want to target. You will be given many options, such as to have your ads appear in just the United States or to have them show in both the United States and Canada. You can also have your ads appear in all countries and territories around the world.

   At this point, you can also add information about any locations that you wish to specifically target. You don't have to market to the entire world. You can select very specific markets. A later chapter includes more details on how to adjust this part of your campaign.

7. Select the language that your customers speak. Your ads would only reach English-speaking users if you just select the English option. Google provides support for a variety of languages including Spanish, French, and Hindi.

8. Enter the budget that you will spend on your ads each day. When you go over your daily budget, your ad will no longer appear on Google for the rest of the day. It will come back online the next day.

   Be advised that you might be charged extra on occasion if you go over your budget. This is because Google calculates its budgets based on a 30.4-day month. Google will multiple your daily budget by 30.4 to determine the absolute maximum amount of money that you would spend on a campaign. For instance, a campaign with a daily budget of $10 will spend up to $304 each month. This is a minimal increase over your expected maximum of $300, but it helps to know this so you aren't confused if this ever happens.

9. Select whether you want your budget to be spent at a standard or an accelerated rate. With a standard delivery method, you will spend your budget evenly. The placement of your ads will be controlled so you won't waste your daily ad budget during the first few hours of the day. Your ads will show up in the morning, afternoon and evening, thus making your content visible to more people.

The accelerated rate means that your ads are going to be fast-tracked. They will appear more often and be more persistent on typical searches. This gives you the opportunity to have your ad out faster, but you are at risk of your ads running out quickly. You can use this if you have a time-sensitive offer and you need to get people to see your ad right now. However, your daily budget could be completely used in just the first few hours of the day depending on how popular your ad is.

10. Determine the bidding structure that you want to use. You can choose the number of clicks you want to get or the conversions involved in your campaign. You will learn more about the bidding options and how the price you will spend will be determined later in this guide.

    You can add information about how much money you want to spend on an individual click. This refers to the maximum total that you will spend for each click.

11. Select the start and end dates for your campaign. You can keep your campaign going for as long as you want by selecting the None option when choosing the end date. It is recommended that you set such dates up for your campaign. When you use the right dates, it becomes easier for your campaign to be run to your liking.

The next points explain the use of extensions. These will be covered in their own dedicated chapter, but at this point, you can add them if desired.

12. You have the option to add some sitelink extensions at this point. You can add these extensions to include additional information on what your site offers. This

only appears when Google predicts that the extensions would be of use at a given time.

A sitelink extension allows people to go to individual parts of your site. This would include a text spot for a link, one or two description lines, and the URL that the link would go to. You can use up to four of these sitelink extensions at the bottom of your listing.

For example, a pizza delivery ad might have sitelink extensions that lead people to sections of a site for information on locations, how to contact them for delivery, or how to reach a carryout service. The added links show that a site has more to offer and can help people to get to specific parts of a site quickly, thus making the link all the more appealing. Remember, these links will not appear every single time someone gets them on a site.

13. You can also add callout extensions to your campaign. A callout extension is one where you will create a short 25-character callout message to people who might be interested in your content. This works particularly with mobile devices and is also optional. It would only work when Google determines that it is appropriate for use at the time. You can choose to have this extension appear at certain times of the day as well.

A callout extension is a small line that appears under the main body of your text. It could include small bits of data relating to whatever you are selling. For instance, a vacuum cleaner store might have a callout that says "Dyson vacuums," "Rug Doctor vacuums" or "5-year warranty" among other things. The key for a callout extension is to let people see what makes a company's listings more appealing.

The content can have keywords that link to your ad set too. Just see that the keywords are relevant to what you are trying to promote.

14. Include a call extension at the end. A call extension is the phone number for you on your ad. This is even more important for mobile phone users as they can tap on a phone icon to directly call you from where they are.

    With this, you can choose to get reports on your calls. This includes information on when people call you based on the link that you have produced. You can also count conversations as calls from your ads. This is perfect if you are trying to reach people by using a certain number.

    A forwarding number can be prepared by Google to help you keep tabs on your conversions and leads through that call extension based on when people call your business.

15. Add additional optional extensions. The extensions are all optional, but they can make your ads more appealing. These are not going to appear every single time someone finds your ad, but they can appear when you are ranked high enough or Google deems your ad to be the best option for an individual user at any given time:

    • You can add snippets of text to your advertisements that show information on the types of products or services you want to market on your site.

- App extensions can be created to post a link to an app that someone can download. This works best for mobile devices and is appropriate if you have an app to work with.

- Message extensions are for mobile devices and allow people to send a message to you. This allows someone in your workplace to respond to any questions or concerns they might have.

- Promotion extensions may include information on any special sales or offers you have. You can add promo codes on this part of your site while also setting up times for when a promotion might be valid.

- Price extensions can include information on what it costs to get certain products or services.

These will be covered later on in this guide. Each has its own quality features to create a layout that will benefit you.

16. Select the ad rotation. You can also select the ad rotation rate based on what you want to promote at a specific time. You can optimize ads that are expected by Google to get the most conversions or clicks so they will air the most.

You can also have your ads to rotate at different points. The lower-performing ads might show up as often as the higher-performing ones. This option can work if you want to showcase various messages, but it might not give you the best possible results.

17. Set an ad schedule. You can get your ad to appear at different times in the day. You can have your ad appear on certain days of the week or even every day, every weekday or every weekend.

    For instance, you can state that you want an ad to appear on Mondays to Fridays from 9am to 5pm. Meanwhile, you can add multiple parameters like having an ad appear on Tuesdays from 4pm to 8pm and Thursdays from 12pm to 6pm. These times are based on the time zone where you are, so confirm that your ad will appear during that timeframe.

    This step ensures that people will only see your ads at certain times of the day or week. This is perfect if you want people to find your content while your store is actually open or when you are available to be contacted.

18. Choose your location options. When you choose your location options, it will be based on people in your targeted location or people who also share an interest in your location. You have the option to target your search toward people who are searching for certain keywords based on what is in a targeted location. You can also choose to exclude people who are in your excluded locations or both people in those locations and those who show an interest in them.

    For instance, a pizza delivery place in Cleveland might choose to market toward the people who are in its targeted area as well as those who are interested. That is, people who search for pizza delivery in Cleveland might get an ad for this place even if one is not necessarily located in that geographic area.

19. Select a campaign URL if needed. A campaign URL is a tracking template. This is the URL that people will go through before they get to your landing page. The template will lead people to a URL that is different from the URL that you have listed on your ad. This is perfect for when you are trying to take advantage of a certain tracking campaign or you are trying to get people to move to a specific landing page.

After completing all these steps, you should have your campaign set up appropriately. At this juncture, you will be able to create ad groups. The next chapter focuses on this part of producing a great campaign.

Chapter 13 – Getting Your Ad Groups Prepared

After you have set up your campaign, you can start working on your ad groups. This should work with many of the keywords that you have chosen at this point. The process of planning your ad groups should give you more control.

1. Provide a name for your ad group. Remember to make each ad group distinct from one another. The different names for your ad groups will make it easy for you to distinguish between each group.

2. Enter the keywords that you wish to use. You will have to add the keywords one at a time. You will need to enter a keyword or keyword phrase and then hit enter after it. This is to let Google know that you are using a certain keyword at a given time. You can always cut and paste any documents you have with keywords you have chosen.

   You can always use certain triggers to focus on specific matches you want to work with. Later in this chapter are details on how to work with various keyword match types.

3. Go to the Get Keyword Ideas section to find ideas based on URLs you enter. Google will look at information on your URL and provide you with keywords as well as details of how many searches people enter each month.

4. You can either save your content or add a new ad group. You can use as many of these ad groups as you wish. Just be certain that each group is different from each other and it has its own focus points.

Keyword Match Types to Use

When you plan your ad groups, you will have the option to use many keyword matches. You can use these to create a better focus on whatever you want to market to other people. These matches include the following popular choices:

Note: The keyword match types listed here go from the least restrictive to the most restrictive. The earlier ones are available to more people, but that also includes people you are not trying to actively target.

1. **Broad Match**

   Your keyword may link up with synonyms, misspellings, or abbreviations among other things. For instance, you could use the keyboard "basketball shorts" without quotations or anything else added. This means your ad may appear on not only searches for "basketball shorts" but also "basketball apparel," "sportswear" and other similar choices.

   This is the most basic type of search to use. This could work if you want to target synonyms and get your content out there to a larger audience. Be advised that this choice will make your content easier to spot on unwanted searches. This could lead to people that you don't want to target clicking on your content.

2. **Broad Match Modifier**

   With a broad match modifier, you will use a plus sign right before the keyword. This means your word or some other word in your phrase will appear at a given time.

In this case, using +basketball +shorts would have your ad appear on searches like "shorts for men" or "basketball gear." The two words are not necessarily going to appear together during each search.

This narrows down your search, but it also focuses on certain words. For example, you might show that you have basketball products for sale and that you're willing to be flexible over where you will show up on a search.

3. **Phrase Match**

A phrase match is when you enter the keyword in quotation marks. The exact phrase will appear with the words together in order at some point in an ad.

By using "basketball shorts," you will have your ad show up on searches for something like "basketball shorts for men" or "plus-size basketball shorts" among other things. Those words in your phrase are found together as you have requested.

This is useful for when you want to highlight a product or service but you know that there are many variables associated with it. For the best results, you should still aim to add more keywords that directly link to the products you are trying to promote.

4. **Exact Match**

An exact match means that the ad will only show when your keyword is entered precisely as you wanted it to be. This involves brackets appearing around the keyword.

When you use [basketball shorts] as your keyword, your ad will only appear when the phrase "basketball shorts" is searched. A search like "basketball shorts for boys" would not qualify. Only those two words that you specifically wanted to use will be included.

However, there are often times when you might get a search result that is rather close to what you originally wanted. This could include something like "shorts for basketball." Google will determine what keywords are appropriate for your exact match.

This is a very restrictive option and works best when you have a very specific product that you want to sell. A vacuum cleaner salesman that exclusively sells Rug Doctor vacuums might use a keyword like [rug doctor vacuum cleaners] to ensure that his site shows up. That keyword would not be seen by anyone except for those who are specifically searching for vacuums from that brand.

5. Negative Match

A negative match is one that has terms that you are trying to omit from a search. You have the option to add a – right before the keyword you are entering. It might be easier to simply go to the Negative Keywords on the Keywords tab on your AdWords control panel and specify what you want to avoid.

For instance, your site for basketball shorts might not offer apparel for tennis or soccer. You could use "– soccer shorts" to ensure that your search will not appear on any searches for "soccer shorts." You will still appear on searches for the specific keyword, but you won't show up for when someone is trying to find details on soccer shorts.

Going back to the vacuum cleaner example, a person might use keywords like −Bissel or −hoover when specifying the keywords. This ensures that the person's site will not be found on searches for vacuums from the Bissel or Hoover. Using negative keywords, in this case, ensures that the vacuums are not promoted improperly.

Adding Keyword Parameters In the Middle of Your Ad Group

It is very easy to use specific keyword parameters added to your ad group:

1. Go to the Keywords section of your AdWords site.

2. Select the campaign and ad group that you want to link to the keywords.

3. Enter each keyword you want to use, but use the appropriate quotes or brackets for your keywords.

4. Click on the Save button after you have added the keywords you've chosen.

You can use as many of these as you wish. You can even get multiple parameters listed in one group if you want.

Planning Negative Keywords

You are going to have to keep some keywords from being visible on a search. Adding negative keywords will ensure that your content is not going to show up when particular keywords are used. You can use quotation marks and brackets to work around your negative keywords to emphasize what you are trying to avoid using in your content.

You have to enter your negative keywords separately from the others you are actively using. The following steps are:

1. While on the Keywords menu, go to the Negative Keywords section on the top part.

2. Select the campaign and ad group that your negative keywords apply.

3. Enter the keywords that you are trying to avoid. For phrases, you have to add the brackets or quotes around them to be more specific.

4. Click to Save that listing of negative keywords.

You can indicate as many negative keywords as you want. Your search will be more restrictive when you have more negative keywords. Be sure those negative keywords do not overlap or clash with any words you are actively targeting.

You can go between the sections on your group that list both the keywords and the negative keywords to compare the two. This gives you a clear picture of what is going on with your content.

You must also keep the negative keywords separate from one another based on the groups or campaigns you have. You might have one campaign that targets very different groups of people who might be interested in keywords that you are trying to avoid on another listing. Be ready to adjust your campaigns based on the keywords you wish to target in individual sets.

Working on your ad group is important to help determine the particular keywords you are going to use. Be sure that you add enough keywords to each ad group. Don't forget to consider how you want Google to read them.

Chapter 14 – Creating Your Ads

Now that you have your keywords for your ad groups ready, you can start creating your ads. You can use individual ads for each ad group. You have to use separate ads for these groups to distinguish them from each other.

You can create as many ads as you want within an ad group. You have to make each of them distinct and unique without repeating the same content if possible. Keeping everything unique ensures that your ads will look attractive and users will not become tired of the content.

Google suggests that you create at least three different ads for each ad group you prepare. These ads should all relate to the theme you are using for each keyword.

1. Select the ad group for which you are going to create a new ad. Each group should be labeled based on the name you gave it and the keywords that you have linked to it.

2. Enter the final URL that your ad is going to link people to.

3. Add the first headline. The first headline can be up to 30 characters. This would be the first thing you see on the blue link. This could include the name of your website or company.

4. Add the second headline. This also has a maximum length of 30 characters. It will appear right after the first headline on the same spot. It can include additional information relating to the original headline.

5. Enter the display path. The display path includes two points that will go past the URL that your link will go to. This should include a URL-like path that gives the user an added description of what is on the target page. The listing will not be the same as the target URL; that URL that people will actually reach is the one that you entered a few steps ago.

   Be concise when entering the points in your display path. You can only use 15 characters on each of the two parts of your path.

6. Enter the description. The description can be up to 80 characters. It can include the keywords that you are using. You can use the preview feature on the right-hand side of the screen to see what your ad will look like on both a desktop and mobile display.

7. You will be given the option to create another ad. The same process can be used here. The main goal is to create as many of these ads as possible so your work will stand out.

8. You can add extensions to your ads, but that is optional and will be discussed later.

When you create your ad, keep the ads diverse and varied as possible. This makes your ads more visible in various spots.

Review Everything

At this point, the campaign should be ready. You will have a full display that includes information on everything you have entered into the program. These include points on what audience you are targeting, the number of ad groups, keywords, and ads you have. You have the option to adjust these later.

There are several factors to consider:

1. Check how the keywords are used in your ads. Are they easy to spot?

   It might be easier for your content to be noticeable if the keywords you are targeting are inside the ads. People will notice them as they are highlighted in bold.

2. Are the keywords you are using integrated naturally? Better yet, does the entire ad read well?

   An ad that has random text in it might not be appropriate for AdWords. Google could penalize you because you did not include content in your ad that is unique and easy to follow.

3. Look at how the content relates to the product or service you are highlighting is worthwhile.

4. The content must directly pique a person's interest.

   Whether it entails asking a question or simply stating a benefit, you must have an ad that makes the reader want to click on your content.

Reviewing your content helps ensure that your work is attractive and is suitable for your campaign and your content appropriate and useful.

Using Ad Rotation

The best thing you can do for producing ads with AdWords is to create many ads so you can determine which ones are working better than others. This will keep your ads fresh and lively. People will be more interested in your work if they see that you have multiple advertisements for the same products or services.

An ad rotation plan allows you to get your ads to be visible to more people as your ads with the same keywords will show up at different times.

You can get ad rotation to work for you:

1. Go to the campaign that you want to adjust.

2. Go to the Settings tab.

3. Select the Ad Rotation option.

4. Click on one of the options that you want to use.

You can choose to get your ads to rotate regularly so that one ad appears for some time and then another airs for that same amount of time and so forth. You can also optimize the rotation for conversions or simply optimize your content by having the ads that Google estimates will get the most conversions appear the most often.

You can also select to not optimize your ads. This means even the lowest-performing ads will run as often as the better-performing ones. This option lets you get your content out to more people, but it might not be the best solution.

The options will vary based on the type of campaign you have and your goal for that campaign. You might not be able to get your ads to rotate evenly.

Frequency Capping

Frequency capping is a feature of a campaign that lets you set limits on how many times an ad will run.

This works for cases where you are trying to make your ads visible, but also to make sure you do not overkill when promoting your work. Having your ads appear too many times in a given time period might actually drive people away.

1. Select the campaign for which you wish to cap the ads.

2. Go to the Settings tab.

3. Select the Frequency Capping option.

4. Determine if you wish to add a limit on viewable impressions.

5. Select the number of impressions that you want to use in a campaign during a certain time period.

6. List the frequency at which these ads will be limited each day, week or month.

7. Select a specific grouping that you want included to be capped.

You can choose to have limits on one of the following:

- How many times ads within your campaign appear on a user's browser; this is regardless of which ad group the ads are found.

- How many times ads in a specific ad group appear; this includes all the ads that are within that group.

- How often a single ad appears; when one ad in an ad group or campaign reaches its limit, another ad from your group or campaign will show up in its place.

This can be useful for any part of your ad campaign. This is to create a better campaign that handles your content correctly.

Chapter 15 – How to Write the Best Ads

So now you know how to create an ad on Google AdWords and how to make that content stand out properly. The process is very simple and lets you showcase your business to more people. However, how are you going to ensure people will actually click on your ads?

When you create a great ad, the Quality Score on your ad will increase. This is a measurement of how well your advertisement reads. When your Quality Score is higher, your ad will more likely show up. More importantly, you will spend less money on each click because Google reads your ad as a trustworthy and viable one to display.

This chapter focuses on some steps you can use to write a great AdWords ad. Use this process to get more out of your content.

Basic Steps

These steps should work regardless of what you are promoting and make your content stand out and be more visible.

1. **Effective Headline**. The headline you use is in blue area that appears at the top right above the URL in green. You can use any kind of headline including one that features your business name and maybe a brief description of what your business offers and incorporates a keyword.

   Create something that immediately piques the reader's interest. You could add a headline that asks a question or maybe creates an interesting proposal.

   Let's say you are selling herbal treatments for dandruff. You could write a headline that says "(product name)

Dandruff Treatment Shampoo" or "Dandruff Treatment Products." An even more interesting headline would be "Got Dandruff?" or "Is Your Dandruff a Problem?". A question would immediately cause someone to view your site as more interesting because you are proposing something valuable to a person who is struggling with dandruff.

Make the headline attractive and that something worth reading is on the other side. Your content has to be useful and gives the reader is going to learn something worthwhile.

2. **Current Headlines**. Consider the content you are adding and decide if it is something that you can use now and in the future. You might have to adjust your ad copy every once in a while to keep the content current. For instance, you might change the words you use based on different seasons or times of the year. Even some statistics relating to how your business operates can be considered.

3. **Be specific**. Don't talk in generalities.

   In the example of the dandruff remedy solution, you would mention the particular products you have. You can explain to the reader that you have dandruff shampoo and conditioner products and supplements to help control scalp issues.

   The problem with some content is that it is too vague. For instance, an ad for an herbal skin care company might say something like "This one ingredient treats dryness." That would be an unpopular ad because it is not actually saying what is being offered. If the company ad says "Learn how aloe vera can treat dryness," this would be a much more attractive headline. A person will want to click on the headline to learn more about what makes aloe vera special and unique.

4. **Wording.** Avoid passive tense words or third-person. The passive tense suggests something happened long ago. Use an active voice to show that something works right now.

   Sentences in the third-person make the ad appear as if you are talking to someone else. Use second-person content to directly contact the person who is reading your ad. Direct second-person messages make the reader feel as though you are talking directly to him or her.

   A description of your dandruff control ad could say "Get rid of your dandruff today! Our shampoo and conditioner products can help you." This directly shows a sense of immediacy while showing that you care about the needs of the reader.

5. **Local or Demographics**. Are you trying to target a specific area or demographic? If so, you can always use words that cater to the group.

   An ad that targets women can include terms that women can appreciate. Maybe the heading can say "Ladies – Struggling With Dandruff?" or "Don't Be the Next Woman to Have Dandruff."

6. **Call to Action.** This is a message that encourages a reader to look at your site. You will use a Call to Action as an open invitation to anyone who wants to read what is on your site. You are showing that what you have to

offer is interesting and worthwhile to your prospective audience.

The Call to Action can include some specific instructions, such as to download an app, buy a product, or sign up for email alerts. This helps you make your content more appealing.

7. **Create Different Ads.** Use multiple variants of your article. You could create one dandruff control ad that focuses on working professionals or another that caters toward women. Maybe another ad might be for people in a certain region.

   When you create more ads, you can get information through AdWords on how many times your ad appears and how many people click on it. You will discover what types of people are likely to review your site.

Each of these steps can help you with doing the most with your content. The next few sections focus creating quality ads.

Working With Trigger Words

You can use trigger words to make certain things memorable and important. Trigger words are words that spark certain feelings and cause a person to want to take action.

Some of the words you can use will focus on the following emotions:

1. **Anger**

   A lawyer might include some trigger words or phrases like "Get the justice you deserve" or "Take back your rights" among other things. These are points that show that target a person who is angry and wants to get legal justice. Anger can be a good motivator.

In the dandruff shampoo example, you can use a phrase like "Sick of dandruff?" or "Is dandruff a pain in the you-know-what?" These tap into the anger that someone has over a condition one has been trying to get rid of but has been unsuccessful.

2. Disgust

Sometimes the one thing that people might be disgusted with is their own bodies. Have you ever taken a look at yourself in the mirror and felt disgusted with something? Maybe you don't like that gut or some stretch marks or other unappealing feature.

You can create an ad that says "Doe dandruff makes you less of a person?" or "Stop that hideous dandruff from making you look unattractive." These give the reader the feeling that one should be disgusted with dandruff and the reader needs to do something about the problem.

3. Value

Some of the best trigger words focus on value. People might be interested if they notice words like "money-back guarantee," "clearance," "discount" or "cheap" because people love to save money.

Value-related trigger words should be chosen based on the overall cost of a product. A word like "money-back guarantee" would be best for more expensive products. Anything labeled as "cheap" might be seen as poor-quality.

4. Simplicity and Speed

Words involving how easy it is to use a product or service is always welcomed. Possible customers for your product or service will want to see that what you are offering is not complicated. Even better, people love something that works quickly.

Some of the top trigger words you can use include "easy," "simple," "fast" or "quick". You might say in your ad that someone can get quick results from a dandruff shampoo by using it for only one week.

5. Premium Words

You can also use some premium words. Some people might be interested in high-end products. Many feel that it is acceptable to pay extra for some high-end item because such a product or service might be better in quality.

You can use words like "premium," "elite" or "VIP" to indicate that a product or service is attractive and of the best quality, and what you are offering is special and distinct.

Incorporate the Features

You should explain some of the features of your products or services when writing your AdWords ad. You must use these features as the USP or Unique Selling Proposition for whatever you are trying to sell to others.

The features of a product or service can explain how a product or service is better than others by emphasizing a certain feature. For instance, a site that promotes a vacuum cleaner for sale might have something in the ad about how the cleaner does not lose its suction or maybe works without chemical cleaners.

No matter what you use as your USP, you must make sure it is distinct so it is attractive and easier to spot and use.

Highlight the Benefits

Does the product have good value? Is it actually going to help one's life and make it easier? A great ad copy will highlight the benefits of the product and if that product or service is worth using.

Explain how the reader can use your product in their daily lives and how it can make their lives better. For a vacuum cleaner, you can talk about how a product is easy to use and makes cleaning a home faster.

Don't mix the benefits with the features. In short, the feature is a quality of the product or service. The benefit is a reason for why someone would buy it. For instance:

1. A feature focuses on what is inside. A portable media player might have a feature showing that it can handle several gigabytes of data.

2. A benefit concentrates on what you will experience. That same media player would have a benefit of being able to handle thousands of songs on one device and play them back anywhere and any time.

What goes into a product is the features and what people will feel about using that product is the benefit.

Offer a Call to Action

You have to encourage a person to move forward and take action. You have to highlight something special relating to the campaign.

A Call to Action can be included and is essential to encourage people to find out why your product or service is worthwhile.

The Call to Action will feature words that encourage people to buy something. You will use many trigger words in a Call to Action like "buy," "download," and "call now" or any other command. The vacuum cleaner salesman might use a Call to Action like "Click now to see how our cleaners will make your life easier" or "Stop worrying about dirty floors! See what we have to offer."

The Call to Action must be directed toward the reader. It must let the reader know that you're going to offer something special to that person.

Your Call to Action can:

- Address a problem that someone has and explain quickly that a product or service will alleviate that issue.

- Work with someone's emotions. Say that a product is something one deserves.

- Be direct and encourage someone to see what you have right now. Using trigger words like "call now" or "click now" or "learn about...right now" can get people to see that you are ready to give them something of value immediately.

- Highlight any bonus offers that you want to include if you have free gifts or special deals.

- Showcase any reviews that people have left. You could say "See what people are saying about…"

- Allow the reader to use their imagination. Say something like "Imagine owning…"

- Explain the specific benefit of your Call to Action. You could say things like "Make your life easier" or "Lower your costs".

Calls to actions do more than let people know what you are offering. They make people open to learning more about your wares. It is up to the reader to decide whether what you are offering is worth learning more about.

How to Organize Your PPC Ad

The PPC ad you plan to use will make your AdWords campaign more valuable and attractive. There are many things that you can do:

1. Focus on the benefits of your product or service.

    The benefits are highlighted first. These are what will interest your clients the most.

2. Create a Feature-Benefit matrix.

    This is a listing of the features you have and the benefits that can be derived from its use.

3. Choose three or more features of your product.

    Each feature will be listed in its own row.

4. Add three benefits to each individual feature.

The three benefits will appear in boxes on the same row as the feature.

For instance, a feature in one vacuum cleaner keeps it from losing suction while in use. The salesman can include benefits, such as the vacuum working efficiently, the vacuum requires less time to operate, it doesn't leave bits of dust or other things behind so that you have to vacuum again.

Every feature of something should have more than one benefit. For the media player listed earlier, the feature of more storage space should include benefits like having the power to store lots of files and not worry about running out of space.

The features of support for an added memory card can include benefits like the ability to have even more storage space or the power to switch from one card with certain types of files on it to another card.

5. Include a Call to Action on each row on your Feature-Benefit matrix.

The Call to Action should be linked directly to the features and benefits. So here's how it would work for the media player:

Feature: Up to 16 GB of storage

Benefits: Carry more music with you, don't worry about running out of space, an entire library in your pocket

Call to action: Get an entire library of music in your pocket with 16 GB of storage.

This Call to Action is perfect as it relates to the feature and benefits. More importantly, the benefit is focused on first. The emotional or personal benefit of the product should be at the forefront to let the customer know that what you are offering is special and dynamic.

Just saying that a product or service has a specific attribute is not good enough. You also have to let the reader know why a product or service is valuable and worth having.

Use Active Verbs

A passive verb indicates something happened in the past. For instance, you might read "We have increased the amount of data storage in our media player." This suggests that something was done in the past. Instead, you might say, "Great, you have more data storage in your media player. So what else have you done?"

A great ad copy would be "Carry your music library with you" or "Bring your music anywhere with our media player." The verbs "carry" and "bring" are active verbs that indicate something can be done now or in the future. In this case, a person can carry their music library anywhere because a media player can store so much data.

Active verbs are perfect for the heading on your listing as well. A link that says "16 GB Media Player" might let people know what is available for sale, but it might not be

An active verb may be used instead to create a more dynamic design that piques the reader's interest. For example, an active verb heading could be "Carry Your Music Anywhere" or "Make Your Music Portable."

Active verbs do more than create an interest. They also double as calls to action. You are letting the reader know that your product or service is exciting that has a special benefit that is hard to duplicate anywhere else.

Keep Each Ad Unique

Don't let your ads blend in with each other.

There are some steps you can use to make your ads unique:

1. Review the individual ad copies you are using in your ad set.

2. Look at how many words are being shared with each ad.

3. Find different terms to use in these ads. This includes replacing any repetitive content with synonyms or other descriptive words.

4. Check the headline and your description lines along with the display URL for each ad. Make sure each part is unique and that you are not repeating words from other ads.

As you will read later, you can arrange for your ads to be rotated while also using individual parameters for how often ads run. This includes limits on how many times an ad runs in a day.

Chapter 16 – Requirements of Your AdWords Ad

You have the freedom to promote many products or services in your AdWords ad. There are many requirements for preparing your ad correctly. Follow these points so that your ad is visible and Google is not going to criticize your work.

Editorial Points

Every ad that goes on AdWords will have its own articles that accurate and include sensible information that is useful. Any ad that offers lots of editorial languages or gimmicky content will be flagged by Google. The service encourages sites that have distinct and detailed content.

For your ad to have a sensible editorial layout:

1. Look at the instructions you are included in your ads. Check on how specific they are.

   Anything that says "Click here!" will be frowned upon because it is not specific. You could say something like "Click here to see what vacuum cleaners we have for sale," or "Check out the assorted variety of portable media players we have for sale from the hottest brands." The latter example is perfect as you are letting people know that your site has portable media players for sale and that you are selling models from big-name companies that people already trust.

2. Check to see if you have gimmicky words. Remove anything that appears to be abusive and is not promoting your product or service.

Words like "Free" or "Cheap" or "Bargain" are very gimmicky and promotional. Avoid these and other similar words.

Google often questions such words because they are associated with spam messages. These include many empty messages that do not add anything distinct or special into the content you are promoting.

3. What types of symbols are you using? Avoid using all-caps words or words that are spelled out with certain symbols. Anyone who tries to spell "Free" as "FR€€" might be questioned by Google because that group could be leading to a that might offer something odd or potentially illegal.

Look at Your Destination

The landing page to your link should be relevant to the ad copy you are using. AdWords can penalize or remove your listing if you use a destination that is not appropriate. Google always gathers information on the landing pages to see that they link properly with the content of the ad.

To have your link compatible with AdWords based on the destination:

1. Check how the display URL you are using relates to your landing page.

    Does the display URL match the content you are trying to market? You don't want your display URL to suggest that people are going to head to a site that offers portable media players for sale only to find car stereo systems instead.

2. Change your display URLs to better reflect the products you are selling.

   Your URL does not have to be the same as the landing page URL. It just has to include information relating to the products or services you are offering for sale. You can use the keywords you are targeting so long as the products or services directly relating to those keywords are found on the link.

3. Determine how keywords might be used in your display URL.

   A good keyword can make your content more appealing and valuable. The words in your URL are more likely to be identified by Google.

4. Remove anything that is under construction or maintenance. Test your landing page to see that it is easy to navigate and is easy to load.

5. Test your landing page on various browsers. These include desktop and mobile browsers and different operating systems. Test your work on as many devices or browsers as possible.

6. Avoid using any sites that have disabled the back button or make it harder for people to reverse or leave.

   Some sites trigger pop-ups or are programmed to keep people from leaving. Google will penalize listings like this. Any site that has menus that pop up before a person tries to close a tab or hit the back button will be penalized.

The main point is to make sure the landing pages you create are easy to access and offers everything you want to promote. Be prepared to use the right standards for getting your landing page created so it will look and work properly.

Technical Rules

You must use these technical rules when finding ways to make your content work to your liking.

1. Use only one website on each ad group.

   When you use more than one display URL domain in your ad group, you will be penalized. Your ad group is only designed to work with one site at a time.

2. Remove audio or video tags from your site.

   These tags are not allowed by AdWords as they produce HTML5 content that might appear blank on some browsers or devices.

3. Remove any child frames on your site.

   Child frames include smaller bits of data that you might conceal in certain spaces on your site. These often add more data to your site, particularly data that you do not want to run at a given time. Get rid of child frames before getting your site running.

4. Replace fonts that might be difficult to read with newer ones that are more legible.

   Some fonts might be hard to read on smaller mobile screens. Google prohibits people from using ads that include content that is difficult to read.

Most fonts that you use in a word processing program are good enough to use in your ads. An easy-to-read site will rank high.

5. Check to see if the content of your target URL is public or private. Remove anything that is private or releases that private content to the public.

   Anything listed as being private will reduce the functionality of a site you are trying to promote. Get rid of anything that is private on your Google site so your work will be easier to identify.

Google has set rules to get your content visible. Be certain when getting Google to work for you that you are cautious.

Chapter 17 – Targeting Specific Geographic Spaces

The online world provides the opportunity to target people in any part of the world. You need to decide who your target audience according to where they are located. AdWords gives you the help that you need for this. You can choose to include or exclude various places in your campaign.

You should consider this if you are running a store or website that targets people in a very specific area. For instance, you might have a roofing company in Raleigh that you want people to be aware of, but you don't want people outside of the Raleigh area to see your ads because those people are not likely to have a need for your service.

With Google AdWords, you can adjust the overall reach of your market by targeting certain geographic locations. The process for targeting these areas is very specific. By working with a smart plan, it becomes easier for your content to be highlighted and promoted appropriately to others.

How to Target Certain Location

Decide on the particular area that you plan on reaching when using AdWords. Google gives you support and numerous options for locations that you want to reach. You just have to enter the specific names of the places you will be targeting.

1. As you start up your campaign, go to the Locations section.

2. Go to the Enter Another Location option.

3. Enter the place that you want to market your product or services.

For the Raleigh example, enter the city name. You will notice several options including both the city itself and the Raleigh-Durham-Fayetteville region. You can choose to target either of these options.

4. Click the Target option on the location that you wish to reach.

   Be sure that the choice is reflective of where you want to conduct your business. This gives you control over how you're going to market your work and make it more visible.

How to Exclude a Location

You should be able to target many places within your search, but you might have some areas that you want to avoid as well. For instance, you might have a business that covers a large portion of North Carolina, but you do not have coverage in some regions of the state. Maybe you don't have coverage in the Asheville or Outer Banks regions.

You can always choose to exclude certain places in your searches. Here is how to exclude an area:

1. Enter the places that you want to target at the start.

   In this example, you would enter the entire state of North Carolina.

2. Add details to any areas that you want to omit.

   In this example, you would have to omit the Asheville market and Dare County, the part of the state where the Outer Banks are located.

3. Click on the Exclude option for each of the places that you want to omit.

For example, your ads would appear in North Carolina in the regions of the state that you can target. The ones that you do not wish to target are the ones that will be omitted from the results page.

As you work with this, Be sure to make the content relevant based on the locations you are targeting.

Using the Advanced Page

The processes you just read about are easy to work with, but they can be made even easier when you go into the Advanced Search box. This can be found in the location search section. The Advanced Search box allows you to enter details on places you want to target and what you wish to exclude from a search. What makes this special is that you will get a full visual representation of what you wish to include or exclude from your work.

This can help you to get a better idea of how well your campaign is to be run. Let's go back to the past example involving the state of North Carolina. You might have excluded Asheville and Dare County from the listing, but you might also notice that your coverage area still includes part of the state that you are trying to remove.

Fortunately, the Google Maps display will reveal information on the specific places that are covered and what are excluded. The targeted locations are in blue and the excluded ones are in red. You can look at your map and find places that you want to add to your exclusions list.

For the best results, enter the entire county or metropolitan area of a place that you want to remove from consideration to get better coverage.

There are some additional points about the advanced page and radius adjustment is one of them.

Radius Adjustments

Maybe you are trying to target people who are within a certain distance of your business. You can use the Advanced Search option to change your targeted area based on a certain radius.

1. Go to the Advanced Search section of the Location menu on your campaign.

2. Click on the Radius option.

3. Enter the specific number of miles or kilometers that you want to target. This would create the radius that you will reach.

4. Enter the specific address where you are based. The drop-down box should give you a specific listing for your search.

You can also go back to the Location option and add or exclude other places from that radius. Maybe your team isn't able to reach one of the towns in that 50-mile radius. You could omit your content from that area by entering and excluding that place.

About the Reach

One point you might notice when adding locations to your search is that there is a reach number on your results. This is an important number as it refers to the approximate number of people who might click on your ads. You must use this total so you can identify how many people are likely to find your ads.

You do not want your reach to be too large as you might end up spending money on clicks from people who are outside of the areas that you are trying to target. Then again, if you target too few people your ad will not be seen by enough people.

The reach number is a specific measurement of how many people in an area are signed onto Google services and are visiting Google-associated sites. This may include both people in a certain area and those who are interested in that location.

For instance, you might be trying to market things to people in the city of Syracuse. You might enter the entire Syracuse DMA region, for instance. This would provide you with a reach of about 1.63 million users. These include people from not only the city of Syracuse but also from nearby cities and towns like Oneida, Oswego, Ithaca and Seneca Falls.

Instead, you can choose to zero in on the city of Syracuse itself. As you are only targeting people within the city's limits, this would produce a reach of about 740,000 people. You can still use the Advanced Search option to add other suburbs like Mattydale or Indian Village if you wish. This would increase the reach and target people in the city and just outside of the city.

You could even go as far as to target a very specific area in the city. Instead of targeting every part of Syracuse, you could just target those who are at Syracuse University. This would have a very small reach of about 60,000. This could work if you have a business near the university.

The main key is to think about who is more likely to use your products or services. Look at where they are located and how far people would travel to use your products or to get to your store.

Reach is to not only make sure the right people see your message but also so you can avoid spending too much money on your campaign on clicks that aren't worthwhile.

Chapter 18 – Linking to Google Maps

When you do a search on Google, you might notice a map on the screen. This might appear on the top of your mobile device or on the right-hand side of your web browser. The map will display information on all the businesses in a local area that relate to a keyword.

This is beneficial for marketing as people can highlight their products and services to others on Google easily. You will find the more local content immediately on the map when you search for something.

People benefit from Google Maps on a daily basis. People are always looking for information on where certain places are located. This provides details of what to find when looking for products or services in their local areas. It is one of the most convenient and beneficial programs anyone could ever use.

You can use AdWords with this feature. You can get a quality keyword added to make it easier for your content to be noticeable and useful.

Get a Google My Business Listing

Before you can get onto Google Maps, you will have to have a Google My Business listing. This listing provides people with details on many things relating to your business, such as:

- Photos of your business

- Photos showcasing things you have to offer

- A link to an official website of your business

- Phone and fax numbers; these include traditional and mobile numbers

- Email contact information

- Daily hours of operation

- Links to social media sites that you operate

- A review site for details of any ratings that people have posted for your business

Some extra things may be included depending on the type of business you run. An auto dealer might add details on the types of cars for sale and the specific brands. A restaurant might include the type of food as well as information on specific entrees available.

These are the steps to get a Google My Business listing:

1. Go to business.google.com to get access to the system.

2. Enter your listing on the network. Be sure to add as much detailed information as possible.

3. Enter the category of your business. Google has a pre-set series of categories as choices for you. Enter a keyword for your business and then look through the categories that come up to see what you need to target. This narrows the search so your business will only appear when someone searches using that keyword.

4. List information on your delivery. Select Yes or No when stating if you are capable of delivering goods or services. A place that does not deliver would require people to visit your location.

5. Confirm the data for Google to review. It may take a few days for Google to confirm your content and put it online.

6. Use a verification code that you can send to Google. You may be told to enter a verification code that you will receive by physical or electronic mail. Google requires this to ensure the person who is signing up for a business listing is actually responsible for that business. It keeps people from having their content or information stolen.

How to Make Google Maps Work

After you have your business listing, you can work with Google Maps. Your content will already appear on Google Maps, but the AdWords system will help you make that content more visible on the maps program.

To get your content visible in Google Maps, you will have to have a brand new campaign:

1. Get location extensions applied to your account. This will be covered later in this guide. It is an extension that will link your business or listing to a geographic location.

2. Apply for a Google My Business Listing if you have not done so by now.

3. Start up a new campaign for your ad.

4. Select a standard or Express ad and then state that you want to get people to reach a physical location. This option opens up many parameters you can use for getting people to come to your physical location. This also opens up an opportunity to get the Google Maps system to start working for you.

5. Target the proper location to which you want to market your content. The location should be close to where your business is. For this, you can select a specific area or a radius surrounding your business.

6. Review the keywords you are using. The keywords you add to your account should relate to the listing you have. They should be competitive and words that someone would realistically use when doing a search.

7. Set up a bid strategy. You can set up bids by location. As you set up your campaign, you must prepare a listing for how much your bids will be based on the physical location your map ad will appear.

8. Confirm all the data on your campaign.

9. You will be asked to send in a verification note. This note will be used for map-specific ads. This is to confirm that you are the one who is running the site for the ad. You might get this verification through electronic or physical mail. When you get it, send the code back to Google. The instructions should be included with the content you are using.

This process will make it easier for you to be visible on Google Maps. This is perfect when you consider how many other places online are using Google Maps to promote your content and make it more attractive and useful.

Key Tips For Using Maps on AdWords

Getting Google Maps to work on your AdWords account is a necessity. Part of this includes knowing how to use AdWords the right way. The following points should be used when making AdWords work for you:

1. Be sure your business listing is as detailed as possible.

2. Review how your business compares with others that might show up on the same search. See that your ad is distinct from others and is unique in some way.

3. Focus on the mobile aspect of your map ads. Most people who use Google Maps work with mobile devices to find information on things near them in real time.

4. Determine how accurate your listing is in terms of where it appears on the map. Always look at how your location is highlighted on Google Maps. Google Maps might not pinpoint your site exactly.

Chapter 19 – Targeting Specific Demographics

The online world is filled with people who have their own interests. Some people might be more interested in particular products or services than others. Younger people, men, and women might be looking online for different things. This is demographics.

In short, every product or service has to target one group or some related groups. Not everyone can be like Coca-Cola or Pepsi and target practically every group with their product.

You must determine the demographics you want to target when using AdWords. Google has a great plan for users of AdWords to help target specific people. For instance, you can target people based on their ages, gender, or household income.

Specifically, you can use different bid options for certain demographics or exclude them from certain campaigns. You can use this for each ad group that you have. You have to determine the types of people that you feel might be more interested in what you are offering.

Note: Be advised that the types of demographics you can target in your AdWords campaign will vary based on the particular type of campaign you wish to operate.

The Main Demographics

There are several demographics that Google AdWords uses when measuring how well certain things are coming along. These demographics are easy to move between:

1. **Age:** AdWords specifies six different age groups: 18-24 range, 25-34, 35-44, etc. and 65+ range.

   You can also target people whose ages are unknown, although you can never tell who is in that demographic. Google uses an array of age groups. You can use this to target younger people in college, middle-age working professionals, or those who are retired.

   Younger children are not covered by Google AdWords. Advertisers on Google are not legally allowed to target their advertisements to younger children.

2. **Gender:** You can target men and women as well as people who have not specified their gender. These include people whose genders are unknown to Google.

3. **Household Income:** This refers to the general spending power that someone has. This section offers six ranges including ones for people in the top 10 percent of spenders in the country and those in the bottom 50 percent. This measurement allows you to target people who might have lots of money if you have something valuable or those who don't have much money and you want to market something cheap or affordable.

   You can also review the combinations that are listed here. For instance, women in the 35-44 age range who earn in the top 11-20% range might be more interested in your product while men in the 65+ age range who earn in the top 31-40% range might not have much interest in your product or service. You can tailor your ads to specific people.

   Note: As of April 2018, the household income option is only available in certain parts of the world. This includes the United States, Japan, Australia, India, and Mexico. This is due to a lack of information on household income reports or that such reports are kept private in particular countries.

4. **Parental Status:** You can target people based on whether or not they are parents. Products for childcare needs can be perfect to promote to parents. You can remove people who aren't parents from consideration. This ensures that only parents can get in touch with you. You can use this option when you are trying to highlight products made with childcare and parents in mind. You obviously cannot market certain toys to children, but you could market them to parents and explain why these toys are beneficial to child development.

How Does Google Identify Different Demographics?

Google gathers demographics from people who are signed into their Google accounts. These include accounts from people who use places like Hangouts, Gmail, YouTube, Google Plus, and other sites that are directly associated with Google.

Your Ad Profile can explain how this content can be gathered and be used. Go to https://adssettings.google.com/authenticated and you will see how you can adjust the ads that you want to see. This is something that many people use when finding information on Google. People can use their Ad Profiles to control their ad experiences so they will not likely to see ads that they aren't interested in. You will notice that you can add topics that you like and ones that you don't so Google knows which ads you want to see which ones you don't.

The Your Profile section of the page is even more important. This includes information on your gender and age. A person can share their age based on a birthday or choose to keep it private. For gender, people can choose to say that they are male or female or if they would prefer not to say. People can even specify themselves as being of another gender. This includes a gender-fluid or transitioning person being referred to as "other" with that person being referred to as "they" or "them" albeit in a singular tense.

The interests that one has and the sites that person visits while online can help determine the parental status and possibly the income that one earns. People can always choose to add their own income data. This includes the disposable income someone might have.

Using the Demographics Section

The following steps focus on the demographics section on AdWords:

1. Go to the Demographics section of the main control panel.

2. Go to the proper section on the top part of the page. There are sections dedicated to individual demographics. You can find sections relating to anything.

3. Review information on the individual demographics based on age or whatever else. You can find information on how many people within a certain demographic have clicked on an ad or how many times an impression was created. Details on what you are spending on your clicks can also be seen here.

4. Visit the Combination section to review details on very specific combinations based on multiple characteristics. You can use the check boxes on the top to omit certain demographics to make the screen a little easier to read.

How to Exclude People

All of the individual demographics will be automatically selected as ones that you can work with. However, not every single demographic is actually one that you will want to work with.

You might have to add exclusions to your advertisements. Maybe the products you are marketing are not appealing to certain people. Do you think that a selfie stick would be useful for people in the 65+ age range? Maybe a luxurious leather sofa is clearly not something to market to someone who is in the lower earning category.

To exclude people from your campaign:

1. Go to the Exclusions section at the top part of the Demographics section.

2. Click on the campaign or ad set you are looking to change the parameters for.

3. Select the specific demographics that you want to exclude.

4. You can also go to the age, gender, household income, or parental status sections and click on the green buttons on each individual entry. You can click the red buttons on the unwanted sections. This is best if you want to exclude a person from one ad group but not from another.

You should only exclude people from your ads when you know who you want to target. You might want to let an ad run for some time to determine if there are certain demographics that are more likely to express interest in what you have to offer and which ones are not.

Dealing with the Unknown

There are often times when people will not list information on their gender or ages among other things. Maybe a person is sensitive about their age. Perhaps a person might not be comfortable sharing their gender or is not concerned about the concept of gender, to begin with. Either way, there are many cases where people will not have their demographics made available to Google.

You can always exclude people who have unknown demographic information. However, you should only exclude the unknown people from your search if you are certain that you have a narrow audience that you want to target. When you exclude the unknown people, you risk excluding a good number of people who might have a genuine interest in whatever it is you are marketing.

This is valuable for you to look into when seeing how society is changing. Working with people who have unknown demographic statistics might be worthwhile when you consider how varied those people might be.

Changing Bid Points

You might have a need to change the bidding process for certain types of demographics. This is for cases where the bids might be too high for one group. This could also happen when you really need to target a particular demographic and are willing to spend a little extra in the process.

To change the specifics of the bids you are working with:

1. Click on the specific demographic box that you want to work with. Be sure you are in the right section before doing so.

2. Go to the Edit option and click to change the bid adjustments.

3. Enter a percentage total for what you will add to or remove from what you are spending. The bid adjustment allows you to increase or decrease your bid total for a keyword by a certain percentage within a demographic. You might spend 20 percent more for people in the 18-24 age range and then 30 percent less for the 65+ range. Maybe you want to spend 50 percent more on women and 10 percent less on men.

4. Click on the Change Max CPC Bids option to change the total value of the CPC bids that you are willing to use. You can choose to set a new maximum total of how much you are willing to spend on each click for a link within a demographic.

5. Go to the Change Max CPM Bids choice to adjust how much you are willing to spend on CPM bids within that demographic. You can increase or decrease this total by any value that you might feel is appropriate.

A Note About Demographics

When working on the demographics for your AdWords campaign, be sure that you are targeting the right people. In many cases, targeting a good number of people will help you to make your content more visible, but that does not mean that every person who sees your ads will want to click on them.

Decide who might be interested in your product or service so that you are marketing your to only the right groups of people. However, one thing that you should do is to allow for your ad to run for a certain period of time before making a decision. You could look at which demographics are more likely to click on your link. At this point, you can start to narrow down your audience. You can omit the groups that are either not getting your ads or the ones that see them but are not actually clicking on them.

You can ensure you don't waste your budget on people who are not actually going to want to see your site. These include people who might click on your site and then decide they are not interested.

Chapter 20 – Creating Audiences

Every advertisement deserves a good audience that is receptive and willing to pay attention. You can create an audience that will be likely to see your ads. An audience is not necessarily based on particular demographics. Rather, your audiences focus more on the sites that they visit and what might be of interest to them.

Audience targeting is a strategy that lets you reach people based on the interests that they show. These include people who have specified in their Ad Profiles that they are very interested in particular things.

This also does well for marketing people based on certain websites that they visit.

Targeting or Observation?

A vital part of creating an audience for AdWords is the strategy you will use to reach people. You can choose to either target or observe the people that you want to have as an audience.

Targeting is a process of telling AdWords where you want your ads to show up at certain spots on Google. This is best for when you have a clear idea of who you are going to market your work to.

Observation focuses more on what you can do at the start of your campaign. As you use the observation option, you will have the ability to look at what your campaign is doing based on where people are seeing your ads. This includes understanding the places that people are finding links and if you use pictures, where the pictures are that they see.

Observations are best for newcomers who are uncertain as to who they should be targeting. Targeting is better for experienced users who know what to expect from their ads.

Creating Your Audience

To create an audience:

1. Go to the Audiences section of AdWords.

2. Select the campaign or ad group that you wish to add an audience.

3. Select either the Targeting or Observation choice.

4. Enter a series of terms or phrases based on how people interact with your business. The system should display information on from where people are reaching and getting on your site.

5. Select the options that are available. Determine the specific types of people that you want to reach.

6. Go to the exclusions link on the top part of the section to set limits as to which audiences you do not want to see your ads.

   You can use exclusions to remove websites on which you don't want your ads to be seen. This is for cases where you want to avoid a certain grouping of people or you know that one group is not going to give you good results.

Chapter 21 – Using the Keyword Planner

Entering the keywords and the right keyword match types that you will use on AdWords will help you to get more out of your ad campaigns. A good idea is to use the Keyword Planner.

The Keyword Planner is a tool you can use to create a better campaign. This works on any ad set.

You can use the Keyword Planner to get as many keywords as you wish. Best of all, you do not have to add individual bid values to each of those keywords if you do not want to. You just have to let the Google AdWords platform include all those things into the same campaign or ad group that you are going to target.

Understanding the Keyword Planner

The Keyword Planner tool helps you identify keywords to incorporate into your site.

The planner assists you with finding keywords that are relevant to whatever you are aiming to include in your campaign. The setup works for people who want to create new campaigns and those who need an extra bit of help identifying keywords that they want to use.

You can also get historical statistics on individual keywords. You will learn what is causing a certain keyword to become popular and how many people have used that keyword at a given time. Traffic forecasts can give you an idea of what is happening in the market.

How to Use the Keyword Planner

The steps for using the Keyword Planner are:

1. Go to https://adwords.google.com/aw/keywordplanner to get started on the Keyword Planner.

2. Enter words or phrases or even a URL that relates to your business. You can enter as many as you want. Google creates drop-down results for each item you enter to ensure that the content you use is accurate.

   Try to include as many things into this section as possible. This should give you a plan for creating a more diverse campaign ad.

3. Review the individual keywords that are listed on the page.

   You will see many keywords including items that are directly related to what you entered as well as some that are so relevant.

   Let's say that you enter "vacuum cleaner". Many keywords will come up like "handheld vacuum," "small vacuum cleaner," "stick vacuum" and many others.

4. Check on the competition involved with these keywords.

   Some of the keywords you will find have a strong competition where more people are linking their sites to those keywords. This requires you to put in more effort and maybe more money into getting your keywords to be visible.

   You will also notice the average number of monthly searches that you will realize from each keyword. Some of the most popular ones have had 10,000 or more searches.

5. Analyze the typical bid values that are attached to each keyword on the listing.

   The bid values included here involve totals based on the low and high ranges for each keyword. Some keywords might be available for as little as 50 cents per click. Others may go up to $5 per click. Google gets this information based on how much money people are willing to place on their bids.

6. Click the checkbox for any keyword you are interested in using.

   You have the option to add as many of these keywords as you want. You may be given the option to select every single keyword that is listed on the screen, but this might not be recommended as some of the keywords might not be relevant to whatever you are trying to market. Review the points for each keyword.

7. Click to add a keyword to a plan.

   You must select the ad group for which you want the keyword to be added. You can also select the keyword to be part of a broad, exact, or phrase match.

8. Click on the View Forecast button.

This should appear on the bottom part of the screen after you add an ad group.

9. Review details on the forecast. This is based on the keywords you are using.

   The forecast is a review of the possible impressions or clicks that you will get from a keyword. It includes a click-through rate that measures the percentage of impressions that will become clicks. The approximate cost per click that you might spend should be listed as well.

The top part of the page includes a full layout of every keyword you will use. The bottom includes results for individual keywords. This gives you an approximate idea of what you might spend on using a keyword. Of course, you can use limits for how much you will spend each day. The measurement just gives you a general idea of what you might spend when using that keyword.

10. Click the Download Keywords file to get a CSV file prepared.

The CSV file will let you save and review the results of your search later. The file format can be as a Microsoft Excel or most other popular spreadsheet programs.

11. Go to the Plan Overview section to get a full summary.

The Plan Overview section will provide you with extra information on not only what you could spend but also where your content will be found. You can get information on the devices that people are likely to use to search for your keywords, thus helping you to configure your ads based on whether a desktop or mobile device would be used for accessing your content.

Details on a location can also be included. This includes information on the most popular places in the country that certain keywords might be used. Naturally, you are more likely to get information from larger markets like the New York, San Francisco, and Chicago markets, but this section is just a rough estimate of what you could find.

The overall process helps you to determine what keywords might work best while giving you details on what you would spend. This is a general guide for what you will do before you start running your AdWords campaign. When used right, it gives you a sensible plan to work with.

You will have to use this feature if you wish to get the most out of your AdWords campaign. The Keyword Planner is designed to give you a clear idea of how well your ads are laid out and how well they can function in your marketing plans.

But What If the Value Looks High?

When you get results from the Keyword Planner, you might notice that you would have to spend a massive amount of money to get certain results. It might say that you'd have to spend $10,000 or more to get particular results within a certain month.

This is just something that Google lists based on what a national advertiser uses. Your results will obviously vary. If anything, you will only spend a fraction of whatever it is Google lists.

In the end, you have the freedom to choose how much you will spend on your ads in one day. You can just spend $30 a day or $900 per month at the most if you are really interested in it. Don't forget that every keyword has its own value, so make sure you look at how you're going to make your content worthwhile.

How Many Keywords Is Best?

The last thing to note about the Keyword Planner is that you have the right to get as many keywords added into your campaign as you wish. You can work with just a few or with lots of them at once.

Although you can easily read how individual keywords work on Google, you have to review how many of these are going to work for you. You must look at how well your keywords are organized based on how relevant they are to your work and many other factors.

You can use about five to ten keywords in most ad groups or campaigns. Use this at the start to see how well your keywords are working and if you are getting enough people to your site. After that, expand your reach with extra keywords.

Chapter 22 – Reviewing Your Landing Pages

The links that you create on AdWords are important, but it is the landing pages that you use that can make the biggest impacts. When you use great landing pages, you can make your campaign more worthwhile. You can also determine if the pages that you are linking your ads up to are useful.

The landing page is the place that someone will first visit after clicking on your AdWords ad. Google can measure how people interact with a landing page after getting there through your AdWords link.

In mid-2017, Google added a feature to AdWords for people to find information on how landing pages are working.

The Value of the Landing Page

You might not believe that the landing page you are using is important to your AdWords campaign. After all, it is not the point that will be visible directly through your AdWords ad. However, AdWords as made landing pages very important in recent time.

When a person clicks on your ad, that person will be sent to a landing page. The person will want that landing page to be relevant to whatever it is they were searching for. The person will want to see that the landing page has content that relates to the keyword, description, and content. When the landing page is relevant to the content being promoted, it will become easier for the content to stand out and work well.

The landing page is often the first impression someone would have toward your business. You need to have a quality landing page that shows people that you have something worthwhile to market.

The quality of your ad will be determined by how well the landing page works. The landing page has to load properly and quickly for it to work well. When a page does not load or is too hard for Google's search engine spiders to go through, it becomes harder for your ad to stand out. The ad will be forced down in rank to the point where you would have to spend extra money just to get your ad considered by Google.

When you look at the landing page section of your AdWords account, you will get details on how people might interact with it and what they will see. You can use the points listed in this chapter to help you get the most out of your content while keeping it outstanding and attractive.

How to Read the Landing Page Section

There are several bits of information that you will see when looking at the landing page on your AdWords account:

1. Mobile-friendly click rate

The click rate refers to how well people might visit a landing page on a mobile device. This includes knowing how well people are going to move from one part of your site to another. This is a vital measurement considering how so many people are getting online with their mobile devices these days.

2. Valid AMP click rate

The AMP click rate is for Accelerated Mobile Pages. This works when you have created a new version of your Google site that works with AMP systems in mind. An AMP site offers a larger cache availability. This makes it easier for people to find content on a site.

3. Click and impressions

This is the number of times that people review your landing page and the clicks people make on that page. This refers to desktop access for the most part and should include information on how well the content you are working with is managed.

4. General costs associated with each click

You will pay more money when more people click to reach your landing page, but this is vital for you to see that your campaign is going in the direction you want it to.

5. CTR or click-through rate

The CTR is based on how well you are capable of getting people onto your site. This refers to how many people will click on your link versus the impressions people make.

Make Your Landing Page Work

It is vital for you to have a great landing page if you want to make your content work. There are several things that can be done to help you get your landing page to stand out and work to your liking.

1. Check that the landing page you use relates to your advertisement.

   The landing page needs to have a layout that matches up with what the ad says. People who notice that the landing page has nothing to do with the ad will turn away and you will lose them as customers.

Look at how the keywords in your ad are related to your landing page. You might have to adjust the page based on something you notice on the page. A good idea is to have the keyword used in your ad to appear in the header of your landing page or on some prominent spot.

2. Explain on your landing page what your USP is. Your USP is your Unique Selling Proposition. This is what you will want the reader to notice above all else when looking at your site. The USP will let your reader know that what you are offering is distinct and appealing.

3. Create a landing page that is mobile-friendly. Make sure the mobile version of your site works. The mobile version of the page should be just as easy to read as the one on your desktop. It should come with the same keyword features, header, USP and so forth.

4. Produce a Call to Action that the reader will notice right away.

   The Call to Action is what inspires people to respond to your USP. You can use a Call to Action button that brings people to a certain part of your site or a website that is attractive or worthwhile.

   It helps to have a Call to Action on the top part of your page where the user will immediately notice it.

5. Make the Call to Action seem urgent.

   You must establish a sense of urgency when getting your Call to Action to work. Your Call to Action can include a message like "Click Now" or "Call Now" or "Order Today" among other things. This shows that you really want people to buy your products or services.

This also gives people the feeling that they need to take action right now or else they might miss out on what you are offering.

6. Offer something that backs up your claims on your landing page.

   People might be interested in looking at your landing page if they notice that you have many claims on it. These claims might come from reviews on Yelp or Facebook or any certifications you have received from the Better Business Bureau among other places. You can also tell people that your products or services were seen in some publication or another form of media.

7. Work with many landing pages for different links. See which landing pages might work better than others.

   These include pages that are connected to specific parts of your site. You can use many landing pages on different ads in your campaign or ad group and then see how well those pages are doing. You might have to change some ads to use different landing pages if the ones you are working with are not running as well as you might wish.

When you use these points, you will notice on your dashboard that you are getting better results and more people watching what is on your site. This gives you a better chance to get people to see what you are offering. Feel free to experiment with your landing pages and to see how well they are run; you can do more with your work if you use them the right way.

Completing a Mobile-Friendly Test

There is one other thing to see how your landing page works with your ads. This is the mobile experience that someone might have with your ad. A mobile site should be very easy to use. It should not be hard to load up or navigate through. Your AdWords ad will have a better ranking if your page is mobile-friendly.

This is vital because many searches and ad exposures come from mobile devices. Having your work visible to people on mobile devices is a necessity for ensuring that your work can be seen.

To see if your site is mobile-friendly, there is a special test:

1. Go to the Google Mobile-Friendly Test page.

   Visit https://search.google.com/test/mobile-friendly to get access to the test.

2. Enter the URL of your site.

3. Allow the tester to review how the site is laid out. This can take some time to complete.

4. Review the results of the test.

5. When the page is deemed to be mobile-friendly, you can submit information on this to Google. Click the Submit To Google button.

   This allows Google to notice that your site is ready for use on mobile devices. Google will interpret your site as being capable of loading up fast on a mobile device.

6. Review the preview on the right-hand side of the screen to see what your site will look like on a mobile device. You can use this to plan your work accordingly.

7. Check if there are any issues with the test. This should be highlighted with an icon on the screen.

Even if your website is mobile-friendly, you might still be at risk of issues where something on your site is not being read properly. In this case, you would have to click on the note to see if there are certain errors detected on your site. These errors might be images or script not reading well. These problems are more likely to appear on older sites or pages that have lots of data that people might have simply forgotten to review.

Chapter 23 – Ad Preview and Diagnosis

Google offers many preview features that you can use during the actual creation process to get an idea of what your ads will look like. This includes help for both mobile and desktop devices.

The Ad Preview and Diagnosis tool will help you identify how well your campaign is running and how well your ad will show up. You can use this with as many keywords as you want.

To get an ad preview:

1. Go to the wrench icon for your AdWords page.

2. Go to the Ad Preview and Diagnosis tool.

3. Check the region that you are targeting.

   You can click on the Location box to adjust the area that you want to target. This will simulate a search that originates from a certain place. This can be adjusted to target the particular areas where you want your ads to be shown.

4. Review the language that the search will use; it should be in English unless you need something else.

5. Select the device that you want your search to work on. You can use either the desktop, tablet or mobile display. These all use different display features and focus on important points relating to the display.

6. Enter the keyword that you want to search for. When you click on the search box, you will be given a specific series of keywords. These should be the ones within the ad groups you have created. You can click on any of those keywords.

7. Review the results of the search.

   The page will come with up with one of two results. First, it may show that your ad does appear. At this point, you will see what the ad looks like while comparing how the ad looks with others. You will also notice where the ad appears versus others on the same search.

   Second, it may say that your advertisement is not showing up. You would have to perform some additional moves to get your ad to appear accordingly.

Chapter 24 – Establishing Ad Extensions

The advertisement that you have produced on AdWords will have everything you want to highlight and more. Have you considered how your ad might look even more enticing when you have the right amount of content?

You can use ad extensions on AdWords to make your work more appealing and more interesting. You might even make your ad look a little better if it contains more detailed information.

This chapter is to help you identify the steps associated with producing such extensions. You must follow the appropriate steps to create the extensions that you want to incorporate into your work. The good news is that there are many great extensions that you can choose from right now.

To get access to these extensions:

1. Go to the Ads and Extensions section of the AdWords interface.

2. Go to the Extensions tab on the top part of the screen.

3. Check any extensions you might have added while setting up your ads the first time. A full list of everything you are working with should be included here.

When you are on this page, you can start adding new extensions to your work. These extensions can give you a little something extra to work with when creating the most intriguing ads on Google AdWords.

Sitelink Extension

A sitelink extension is an additional link that you will post somewhere in your ad. This link will go to some spot outside of the main landing page that you included at the start of the setup.

Let's say that you have a site that offers home theater equipment for sale. You can have the main link on your ad go to the front page of your site. After that, you can produce multiple extensions that showcase other things that you want to highlight. You can have one extension showing that you've got sections on your site that sell subwoofers, tweeters, speaker boxes, control panels, wires and much more. A person can immediately click on one of those links to be immediately led to a certain section on your site. This makes it easier for someone to find a specific place on your site.

To add sitelink extensions:

1. While on the Extensions tab of the Ads and Extension section, click on the Plus sign and select the Sitelink Extensions option.

2. Select where you want your extension added.

You can add this to your account, campaign, or ad group. After selecting an option, you will have to select the specific group or campaign. A pop-up box should help you choose what you will use.

3. Choose to create a new sitelink.

4. Enter the heading that a person will click on. This can be 25 characters long.

5. Enter the first description line. You can add up to 35 characters here.

6. Add a second description line of the same length if desired.

7. Add the final URL that the sitelink will move to. Make sure it matches the rest of the content on the landing page.

8. You can also add a tracking template. Click on the Sitelink URL Options section and enter the website that the tracking template will be added to.

   A tracking template, in this case, is where your tracking information will be added. You can use this by linking the sitelink extension to the main page that your ad group or campaign is linked to. You can use to track how well people are accessing the content on your site. There is also the option to use a different final URL for mobile use.

9. Go to the advanced options tab to add extra details.

   You can choose to have your ad to appear on a mobile device over others if needed. You could also select the dates when you want your extension to appear and the hours of the day that you want it to show up.

10. After you have created your new extension, go back to the sitelink extension creation menu and create another extension for the same ad group. You can have up to four of these extensions added to an ad group.

11. Test the content by using the preview box. Make sure the four ads you are using are linked to each other on the same listing.

If the ads are not appearing together, you might have to go to the Use Existing section and click on all four of the extensions that you wish to utilize in this case.

Sitelinks are beneficial because you can quickly update them on AdWords. You can change them around on your control panel when you've got new products to sell or if you have certain promotions that you wish to highlight. You can even use these in the Analytics section of your page to see which links people are responding to the most. This gives you an idea of what people are looking for when finding your site, thus allowing you to change your keyword strategy as you see fit.

These sitelinks are free for you to ad. The only thing you will spend is the cost per click associated with people clicking on those links. The cost per click should be the same as that of the main link for your page. Be aware of this as you plan your efforts.

Notes About Sitelink Extensions

Do not go overboard creating sitelink extensions. Your desktop listing will only show up to six at a time. A mobile version will only air four. Make sure that the content being introduced is relevant and worthwhile.

Also, each description and heading you use will have to be as concise as possible. Only make one point with each description. This should be good enough to let your user figure out what you are offering.

Callout Extension

The callout extension on your ad is designed to let you include more text about your business. This can be found underneath the description you are using. It adds an extra bit of information and can give you a good listing that people will be more interested in.

The callout will appear under the description on the desktop view. It will appear immediately after the description on the mobile version and might even appear on the same line as the rest of your content if needed.

1. Go to the Callout Extension section of the AdWords page.

2. Select the ad group or campaign that the callout will appear on.

3. Enter a new callout text. This can be up to 25 characters long.

4. Use the advanced options to determine when in the day or week your callout text will appear.

5. Click the Save button.

You can also go to the Use Existing section to select a specific callout that you have used on another campaign or ad set. The callout will appear throughout the ads in the same campaign or ad set unless you adjust them individually. You can always remove the callout from individual ad groups through the control panel or even add them to other ones if you prefer.

What Should Your Callouts Include?

A callout needs to be informative while allowing people to be more interested in whatever you are highlighting. A callout extension can include:

- A specific selling point that makes your work a little more interesting.

- State something briefly that lets customers trust you. You might promote a money-back guarantee, a special warranty, free returns, free shipping, or a trial that lasts for a certain length of time.

- Explain new products you have for sale. Stating that your site is updated or has new inventory on hand will pique anyone's interest.

Be as specific with your callout as possible. Make sure it fits within the character limit that Google uses.

Structured Snippet Extension

Do you have very specific things related to your products or services that you have for sale? If so, you can use a structured snippet extension. This will appear beneath your text as a special header.

For instance, you might be trying to sell different types of home theater equipment to your customers. You can have a structured snippet that says "Types: Subwoofers, Tweeters, Bass Speakers, Control Panels." This shows that you have specific products for sale. Best of all, these might work well if you are using these as keywords for your listing.

1. Go to the Structured Snippet Extension section of the Extensions menu.

2. Select the ad group or campaign that your extension will be added onto.

3. Select the header type that you will use.

Google has many header types for you to choose from. These include items like brands, amenities, courses, models, types and so forth. The header types will vary based on the information you have provided to Google about your business and what you are trying to get out of AdWords.

4. Enter individual items into the values. You can use up to 25 characters for each of these values.

5. Click the Add Value button when you need to add any extra values outside of what is already listed on the main page.

6. Use the advanced settings option to state when want to get your ad to appear.

The sitelink extensions will appear as a third line under the description and the callout text on a desktop browser. They will also appear immediately after the callout text on a mobile display. Refer to the preview for information.

Tips for Snippets

To design your snippets:

- Think about the items that people are more likely to search for when finding your site. Use those points as snippets if possible.

- See if your keywords can relate to the snippets you are using. Your ad might be easier to spot if people can notice your snippets are online.

- Keep the snippets distinct from one another. Make sure the reader can easily distinguish one from the other. Do not use too many similar characters or words in each snippet or else they will start to blend.

Call Extension

Do you have a phone number for people to use to reach you? Use the call extension feature to add that number. This is perfect for when you're trying to reach people through their mobile devices. You will not only have your phone number listed but your target will have the option to click on the number to call you right away.

The phone number will be listed next to a telephone symbol on the bottom part of your ad when on the mobile version. For the desktop, your phone number will show up next to the green URL you have added near the top.

1. Make sure the phone number you are using is active. Test it yourself if you have to.

2. Select the campaign or ad group that your phone extension will go onto.

3. Enter the specific phone number you will use.

   You must also specify the country that your phone number is linked to. This is to ensure that you will have a clear display of your phone number. American and Canadian users can use the same ten-digit layout with a three-digit area code, but people in Australia would use a two-digit area code with eight numbers following.

   Also, people from outside the country of your number will notice a plus sign showing the calling code that will be used: +1 works for the United States, American territories, and Canada, +61 is for Australia, +45 is for Denmark, +54 is for Argentina and so forth.

4. Choose whether you want to activate call reporting for your extension.

   Call reporting lets you review how your call extensions are working. This includes reviewing cases when people might click on a phone link on a mobile device. A Google forwarding phone number will be added to your call number if you choose this. This number will record information on the calls that come in. You can get information on the details of each call including how someone managed to see the phone number they just dialed.

On a related note, this may work to report information on the phone numbers used to call you. For instance, your reporting setup might show that you are getting lots of 773, 630, 312, and 815 phone calls. These are calls from the Chicago area. You can use this information to tailor your advertising to target more people in the Chicago area because your ads are obviously targeting people in that region based on how so many of them are calling you from those area codes.

5. Select the option for how you will get the conversions counted.

   Your conversions can count as calls from the ads that you are using. You can also click on the Manage Conversions listing to go to the Conversions menu. This section of AdWords will be covered in a later chapter.

6. Select the device preference that you want to use for your ads.

   It is best to click on this so that your phone number appears on mobile ads. This ensures that your phone number will be more likely to appear on mobile ads than anything else.

7. Finally, add advanced options for when your ads are going to appear. You can use this when you are going to show people that you are available.

The good thing about a call extension is that it immediately allows people to dial your number. This is provided that your number is listed directly on a mobile device or a computer that can handle real-time phone calls. The simplicity of the extension ensures that someone will click on your content and use it right now.

<u>Added Points for Call Extensions</u>

A good rule of thumb is to trigger the ad to appear during specific hours of the day. For instance, you might be open from 10am to 6pm on weekdays. You can select to have your phone extension appear only during those specific hours.

Test your number and see what happens on a different line. Make sure the number provides the user with a response as soon as possible. The best thing to do here is to allow for an actual person to be on the other line. This might be more personal than just having an automated message appear.

Message Extension

Text messages have become a popular way for people to communicate. By using a message extension, you can get people to send text messages to you. This allows people to get in touch with you and to ask you questions that you can respond to as soon as possible.

The message extension is designed to only work on mobile devices that offer texting features. Someone will touch the extension that shows as a speech bubble on the side. This will open up a listing that lets someone enter their phone number while sending out a specific message.

After you get that message, you will have the ability to respond to the person who sent it. You always have the option to directly call that person back if desired too. This can even work if you have an auto-responder tool that will respond to the messages people send you, although you might have to watch for the parameters that come with a message.

1. Click on the message extension option.

2. Choose the ad group or campaign you will use.

3. Enter the phone number that the message will go to.

   You can use the same phone number you used for the call extension if desired. Either way, the phone number being used must match the extension you are working with.

4. Enter the extension text. This can be up to 35 characters long. This is the content that the user will see next to the speech bubble that appears.

5. Enter the business name - up to 25 characters. The business name will appear as the first thing on the text after someone taps on the speech bubble. This includes details on the entity that the text will be sent out to. (The phone number that you specified will also appear around the top of the message.)

6. Enter the message text of up to 100 characters.

   This is the message that your user will send out to you. The message will be automatically added to the messaging app. Your user has the option to adjust the message or to send something else to you.

7. Don't forget about the advanced timing options. This can also work for cases where you want someone to get in touch with at a certain time.

Try to use precise timing based on when you are available or when someone can be there to respond by text as soon as possible.

Although a separate auto-responder program can help with sending data out, such programs are not always perfect. Having someone on hand to help send a response to a message is always a good idea.

Message reporting must be turned on for you to get information on the data of the people who are sending you texts.

Location Extension

You will have to have your AdWords account link to a Google My Business account for you to use the location extension. When it is used, people will notice the location of your business. This is a necessity when you are trying to make yourself visible on Google Maps or if you just want to get a map ad prepared.

Your location extension is separate from a map ad. Rather, it would go alongside a traditional ad. The big advantage is that the ad will be easier to find in a local area.

The great thing about a location extension is that it caters to people in your area. That means a person who is a few miles away from your place of business could get a search result featuring your business in particular.

To get a location extension:

1. Get your Google My Business Account set up. Refer to earlier in the guide for details.

2. Link your My Business account to your AdWords account.

3. Go to the Location Extension section of the extensions menu.

4. Click the option to link your business ad group to your My Business account.

5. Whoever operates the My Business account will be given a message about confirming the content.

   In most cases, this would be an email that requires the operator to dial a phone number and enter a code. Depending on the situation, the process might require sending the code by mail, but that is not often the case.

6. After the confirmation goes through, Google will spend a business day or two reviewing everything once more before your link is activated.

At this point, your content should be available for use on AdWords. Your ads will link to a physical location, thus ensuring that they might be easier to find when people are near you or enter keywords relating to that location.

Be advised that this will require a lot of work setting up a Google My Business Account. Such an account must be set up so your content will be easy to read and use. This is also to explain the immense amount of detail relating to your business that you wish to highlight. People are more likely to trust your business when you offer more details about it. The odds are you will get a better ranking on AdWords if you can get a quality listing set up on it too.

When Does This Work?

Anyone can create a location extension, but it is best to do this when you've got a physical location that is fully dedicated to your business. For instance, you might own your own athletic shoe store and you want to let people know where it is located. You could link your work to keywords like "Basketball shoes for sale" or "running shoes for sale" or something more specific like "running shoes for boys" or "basketball shoes size 18 and larger".

When you use a location extension, your location will be linked to those keywords. This means that someone who searches for basketball shoes size 18 or larger will quickly get a link to your ad alongside map information on where it is located.

The copy of your ad would be a little different from the one you use on Google Maps because the map listing is just a small part of what is offered.

Where Does the Extension Go?

Your location extension will appear on one of many places on AdWords:

- It will appear on the Search Network with a little map on your ad with the specific address. This is provided the address is listed in the My Business account.

- It may also appear in the Display Network if you have a picture to use. This might simply just be a map display that shows the location of your business. That is, you might not need an ad designed specifically for the Display Network to get your content to appear on the network itself.

169

- This should appear on Google Maps, although the content of a traditional ad might be different from one optimized for Maps.

- Video ads can display your extension if you have a video, but it may also just be a brief pre-made presentation by Google that lists where your location is on a map.

Try a location extension when getting your ads ready. Always be sure the My Business account that you link to it is fully accurate and has enough content.

Affiliate Location Extension

Are you trying to sell a product that is available at various different retailers in a local area? If so, you can use an affiliate location extension to let people learn more about a specific location that you want people to hear about.

A location extension lets you reach customers within a local area. This works for retail stores although Google has an option that works for auto dealers.

An affiliate location extension works with a simple process. When someone searches for your product or service on Google, your ad will appear with information on a location that you operate. The results might vary if any added keywords based on a certain physical location were included in the search.

This is perfect for when you want someone to go directly to a physical store to buy something. A user can even click or tap on the location extension to get directions. This feature works best for mobile users as a person can use the information on one's location in real time.

This also works on the Display Network or on YouTube. Your display or video ad can appear alongside a location extension. The user who sees the ad will click on the directions icon.

With an affiliate location extension, you can get people to find your location with ease. But this will only work if you have multiple locations.

1. Specify the retail chain where your products are sold. Click on the country and then find the business that has your products.

2. If you have something that you sell at certain auto dealerships, select the Auto Dealers option. After that, look for the specific vehicle company dealers that have your product for sale.

This is a valuable option but must be used with caution. You might have to go to your affiliate location feed to adjust the settings for how your product is available in certain places.

Also, this feature is limited based on what you can highlight. Google only has a handful of countries listed. For the United States, people can find more than 80 retailers. These include convenience stores like AM/PM, 7-Eleven and Circle K. Larger retailers like Best Buy, Dick's Sporting Goods, and Home Depot. Also included are grocery chains like Harris Teeter, Publix, and Safeway. Naturally, smaller local chains may not be found.

For the United Kingdom, you can find retailers like Asda, Bonmarche, John Lewis, and Tesco. In Canada, you can use options like Bell, Canadian Tire, London Drugs, The Beer Store, and The Source.

There might also be cases where certain retailers are found in multiple countries. You have to specify each individual country. For instance, you could say that your products are at Best Buy retailers in the United States and Canada. You'd have to select the Best Buy option for each of those two countries separately and include them in the same ad.

Adjusting Specific Locations

While this extension is useful, you probably are not actually offering your product at every location of a certain chain. For instance, you might have a product available at CVS Pharmacy locations, but that does not mean every single CVS location in the United States will have your product.

You can use your main affiliate location feed to adjust details on the particular locations that carry your product.

1. Start by making sure the advertisement you have is geared toward the right spots.

   If you only have products for sale at certain stores in specific locations, create an ad that targets the locations you are choosing. Keep the location as narrow as possible so you don't go overboard.

   At this point, the extension will only be for the locations of a chain in the area that you have specified.

2. Click on the wrench link on the dashboard.

3. Go to the Business Data section.

4. Click on the Main Affiliate Location Feed link.

5. You can review all the locations of a particular business that carry your product.

You can find individual locations based on state, postal code etc.

6. Click on a column to sort the locations in an area.

7. Select the individual locations that you want to remove. Click on the boxes for each of those locations.

8. Click to have those locations removed from consideration.

Only the locations that you are actively going to target will appear. For instance, you can remove all the CVS locations except for ones that are within a certain radius of where you are based. Be sure to check the individual locations listed.

Of course, the ads that you use will be more likely to be targeted to people who are in the geographic areas that you are trying to reach based on your settings. By configuring the locations you are highlighting on this extension, you will zero in on certain spots while keeping people from being misled into thinking that a specific retailer has something you are offering when in reality it does not.

Price Extension

Everyone always wants to find a good deal. You can highlight individual products or services by using price extensions.

This is different from a shopping advertisement which will be explained later. A shopping campaign is a completely different feature that involves an image.

A price extension will appear near the bottom of your ad listing. This will include information laid out horizontally. A mobile user might have to use his finger to move the layout around to find all the price listings being offered.

1. Select the campaign or ad group that your price extension is for.

2. Enter the type of price extension you wish to use.

   You can use this to highlight product tiers, certain brands and so forth. Select the option that you want to promote the most. If you have a web hosting service that offers several tiers of hosting solutions for customers, select the Product Tier option.

3. Specify the currency that you will use. The American dollar should be the default.

4. Enter the price qualifier. This refers to how the prices that you will display are listed. You can show prices available in three forms:

   - Prices from – the prices go from one total to something higher. This is when you are listing the cheapest option in a certain field.

   - Up to – the most expensive price for something in a field.

   - Average – the average price of something you are offering in a particular field.

5. Enter as many price extension items as you wish. Add a header at the start. This header can be 25 characters long.

6. Specify the price you want to use on your listing.

7. Add a unit if desired. This is when you are charging by the hour, day or month etc.

8. Enter the description of the price. This is limited to 25 characters.

9. Add a final URL. This is where the price listing will lead a person.

   The URL will appear at the top of the ad. Tap or click the header to go there.

10. Include a final URL for mobile users. This should be different from the URL used for desktop users.

    This option works well when you've got a mobile-optimized website or you simply want the user to go to a different part of your site.

11. Click the Add a Price Extension Item option if needed.

    You can use as many price extensions as you wish, but you should try to set a limit.

12. Enter the tracking information to help record information about people going to your site due to the price extensions you have added.

A price extension will only show up when your site is on the top of the listing. This happens when your site is deemed the most suitable for users to see.

Also, you should know that you will be charged when people click on the URLs that you have added here.

Works With Merchant Center

The best thing to do to get a price extension ready is to link your account to a Merchant Center account. This records information on the products you are selling and the prices you have entered. You can even enter events where the prices will change at certain times in the year. You can use the Merchant Center to highlight anything you wish to offer.

You will learn more about the Merchant Center later in this guide. Of course, the Merchant Center would work best for a shopping campaign.

<u>Price Extension Tips</u>

A price extension is a convenient feature, but you should not have too many. Three or four should be good enough.

Each URL on your listing should also be unique. Allow those URLs to go to certain sections or to product pages based on what you are listing. Do not repeat URLs on your price listings or else the site will appear repetitive.

App Extension

Your business might have a special app that you want to offer to people to download.

You can use this to highlight programs for Android and iOS. When you enter the extension, a mobile user will get a link at the bottom of the ad telling them to download your app.

Note: This is different from an app campaign, which will be covered later. The app campaign is designed to directly get people to download an app or make in-app purchases. This also focuses on mobile devices and would probably do best with mobile ads.

To use an app extension:

1. Select the ad group or campaign that will include the app extension.

2. Select the platform that your app is on. You can choose from an Android or iOS setup.

3. Enter the name of the app you are marketing or the package name.

   AdWords will give you results based on what Google Play or the App Store states. Be specific so you can find the app.

4. Click on the app that is listed on the screen. Google will create a proper link that will allow a person to download the program by tapping on the link.

5. Enter the link text you want to use. This can be up to 25 characters long.

6. Select if you wish to exclude tablets or not.

   By clicking on this, your app extension will not appear when someone is using a tablet. Use this for cases where the app is designed specifically with a mobile phone in mind and not for a tablet.

7. Use the tracking and scheduling options on this if you wish.

8. Click on the Save button.

You will be charged for each time someone downloads the app. Also, a user would have to confirm a purchase if the app being downloaded costs money. Watch for what you are willing to spend on your ad and that you price it lower than what the total value of the app is if possible. This includes details on any in-app purchases that may be made.

You will have to use this extension twice on the same ad set if you have an app that works on both Android and iOS devices to ensure that your content can be seen on both devices. Your app will be programmed differently based on the specific operating system it is on.

AdWords does not offer this for Blackberry or Windows Phone apps as they are not as prominent as the Android or iOS options.

Promotion Extension

The last of the special extensions to use is a promotion extension. Use this when you are trying to promote a special sale or offer.

With a promotion extension, you will see a message at the bottom of a desktop display showing that you are selling something with a special deal attached to it. This includes the word "Deal" in bold text next to whatever it is you are promoting.

For a mobile display, a price tag will appear at the bottom of the ad.

1. Enter the ad group or campaign to which this applies.

2. Specify the occasion of the ad.

This will change the "Deal" listing to another message that shows a special deal based on the time of the year. You can say that your offer is a back to school deal, a Black Friday or Cyber Monday deal, or a holiday like Christmas, Halloween, Valentine's Day or many others.

3. Enter the type of discount you are promoting. This should specify a monetary or percentage-based discount. You can also promote a maximum discount (up to 30% off, up to $50 off, etc.).

4. Enter the percentage or monetary total that is a part of the promotion.

5. Enter the item you are promoting. This can be up to 20 characters long.

   You can list either a specific item or a certain type of item. You could also say someone will get a deal off of one single item or an overall purchase. Don't exceed the character limit.

6. Add the final URL. You can use the same URLs of the header or a new URL that links to a page that offers the product you are promoting.

7. Add additional promotional details.

   You can add a message at the end stating that a deal is a certain value total. The message could include $30 off an order over $100 in value, for example.

   A promo code can also be added here. You add a specific code that triggers a special deal. You'd have to keep the promo code specific and make sure there are no typos.

8. Set up the dates that your promotion will apply.

   Enter a start date and an end date. Your advertisement will stay online with no end if you do not enter any specific dates. Like with the other extensions, you still have the option to use advanced settings to let the sale offer appear during certain times in the day or week.

   Be sure to add the appropriate times for your campaign. You need to keep the extension running only when you know it will take place.

How to Add and Remove Extensions to New Ad Groups

All of the ad groups that you have created can benefit from different extensions. Maybe you have some extensions from an older ad group or campaign that you wish to incorporate into a new ad group.

To move the extensions over to the newer ad group or campaign:

1. Go to the proper ad group or campaign that you wish to review.

2. Click on the Extensions tab for that ad group.

3. Click on a box next to an extension that you wish to use.

4. Go to the Add To section and select the specific spot that you want to copy the extension onto.

5. When you are aiming to remove an extension, just click on the extension in question and go to the Edit section. Select the Remove option to get the extension removed from that ad set or campaign.

Be careful when adding or removing content. If you are not specific enough, you might add the same extension to unwanted groups. Look at the specific ad groups or campaigns that something belongs to before deleting it. You might remove something from every campaign or group you are using in error. It is still easy to replace and add it back again later, but you must still be cautious.

Don't forget to use the preview feature when adding or editing extensions to see how the ads in your ad group will look. You can switch from the desktop display to a mobile one. This adds a good setup for making your content stand out.

Experiment with as many of these ad extensions as you wish. When you work with all of these extensions, you will notice that it is very easy to get your ads to stand out and look their strongest.

How Many Variants Work?

You can use as many variants of these extensions as you wish. For instance, you can choose to have multiple message extension feeds that include different bits of content on them. This includes different messages that have their own specific message texts or extension texts added to them.

Whatever you choose to use, you must see that the extensions are laid out carefully and that you can track them. They must all lead to the proper websites, phone numbers, app pages or anywhere else that you want people to see. This ensures that people will have access to your content correctly.

When Google Chooses To Air Certain Bits of Content

Although the ad extensions you can use are appealing, Google is not always going to show every one of these. One extension might be visible while another is not. This could be based on your scheduling or on the number of extensions that you are using.

There are four points that Google considers when it chooses to air your extensions:

1. The layout of a web browser or mobile device will be considered first.

   Google will look at how well your content appears on a certain device or browser before deciding what will appear. You might see that you only have a few sitelink extensions appearing at a time. You might have four extensions, but only one or two might be showing. This is because Google sees you are unable to use certain extensions in a particular fashion.

2. Your ad rank is critical.

This is a point that will directly influence how well your ad appears. Your ad rank will be judged based on the quality of the content and the landing page linked to it. Even the context of a search will play a part in your ad rank. This will be discussed later.

AdWords needs your rank to be at a certain level before any of your extensions can be seen. You might have to get your ad rank to increase or to even spend more on your bids to get your ad extensions to be visible. When your content is at the top of a search engine, it becomes easier for your content to be seen.

3. The positioning of your ad is vital to deciding how your extensions will show.

Your ad extensions will be more likely to appear when your ad is in a better position. This includes a position where the ad is at the very top. There is a chance you might be competing with multiple advertisements on the same Google search. An ad located on a lower position will not be likely to have as many extensions on display.

4. The total number of extensions you are using will make a difference.

You must be cautious when looking at the number of extensions involved with your message. When you enter an auction with AdWords, you will notice the most powerful and popular extensions on your program. You can review which extensions are more likely to appear and what is doing well.

You can always use your Analytics feature to see which extensions are performing the best. This includes details on how often they appear and how often people might interact with them.

Tips for Using Ad Extensions

As attractive as these ad extensions are, you must be careful. Here are some tips to make your extensions stand out.

Keep the descriptions you are using on these extensions short and use the keywords.

1. Always review the individual Analytics for all the ads you are using.

   The Analytics will show when your ads are being exposed to people and how often people act upon them.

2. Watch for how your headings lead people to certain places.

   The headings in your extensions, particularly your sitelink extensions, should all go to distinct places. Make sure each of these extensions includes information that expands upon what your main landing page features.

3. Watch for any dead links on your site.

   Dead links can hurt your extensions. When you remove a page or change something, you would have to remove any extensions that would lead people to dead links.

4. Always review the ad policy guidelines.

   This may sound like a broken record, but every extension you use will be subjected to the ad policies of Google for AdWords.

5. Do not assume that you have to remove extensions to get your content to be more visible. Deleting any of your extensions is not necessarily going to make it easier for you to have your content seen by more people.

The excitement that comes from using Google's extensions will help you get your AdWords listings to be more valuable. You will not only make it easier for your content to be visible but also give people a better idea of what you are offering. You just might get more people to click on your ad when you use enough of these extensions.

Review Extensions

You might have noticed on some Google listings that there are review extensions. These include information on what people might say about a site. This can include a quote followed by the author.

Although a review extension adds some credibility to any site, AdWords discontinued review extensions in early 2018 to streamline the AdWords experience and the extension option was not as popular as other choices. The ads that have review extensions are all ones that were created before the extensions were discontinued still appear on those listings.

Chapter 25 – Automatic Ad Extensions

The last chapter was all about the ad extensions that you can use. But all of those extensions were ones that you would have to add on your own. You can use additional ad extensions that are automatically incorporated into your ads.

Google AdWords uses automatic ad extensions to highlight your content in a dynamic fashion. With this, you will have your ads feature bits of data based on other things that are linked to your site or account.

On the surface, these extensions should be appealing. They will give customers more information on your business based on many things that are highlighted on your account. But there might be times when you want to hide that content. Perhaps you might want to focus more on the extensions that you created yourself.

Whatever you want to do with these extensions, you must notice what you can do to get your content to move forward and work strongly and without issues.

Types of Automatic Ad Extensions

There are six automatic ad extensions that may link to your site based on what Google has found on your site. These could help make your site more viable and appealing to customers, but you might have to opt out of these. The process for opting out of automatic ad extensions will be discussed in the next section.

1. Consumer Rating

   Ratings are based on what people think about you on customer surveys. These surveys include many categories relating to how your business operates. The consumer rating is ranked on a score of one to ten. This will include several total measurements that can be a challenge to work with or adjust on your own.

2. Previous Visit

   A previous visit extension is for those who have looked at your site in the past. The problem is that some people might be uncomfortable with having their data being visible. While a person can remove their tracking cookies and cache from a mobile or web browser, this could still be distracting to anyone who sees it.

3. Seller Rating

   A seller rating lists information on how much people like your store based on prior transactions and the ratings that people have given your site. This is based on a five-star rating from StellaService, Google Consumer Surveys, and many other places.

   A good star rating can be useful when you're trying to make your content appealing to more people. It will be harder for people to get onto your site if your rating is too low.

4. Dynamic Sitelink

   This next automated link is interesting as it offers a link to a popular content or section of your site. This is valuable if you have something that is attractive and worth discussing. At the same time, you might not have the ability to control the content being used in this case. You might have to adjust the way your content is listed.

5. Social Extension (For Google Plus)

   This page lets people get in touch with you and see more of what you have to offer. Think of Google Plus as a social media contact site for use on the search engine. The social extension feature will list details on how many people on Google Plus have liked, or rated your site with +1'. This includes a specific number of who is being offered.

   While Google Plus can be useful, not everyone will focus on this. Opting out of a social extension can help you remove this issue.

6. Dynamic Structured Snippets

   You already learned about creating your own structured snippets as an extension, but you can also use dynamic structure snippets. These are produced automatically based on what Google has identified to be best for your site.

   A dynamically structured snippet will list information on what Google has found to be relevant on your site. This includes details on any sections that might be more popular than others in the listing.

   You can control these snippets by adding your own structured snippets to your ad listing before Google can create dynamic ones. That offsets the automated ones that Google wants to establish on your listing.

All of these automatic extensions are compatible with the manual extensions you might have added to your content. These extensions will appear based on what Google deems is appropriate to display. This is based on the quality of your ad and where it appears on a search.

When Are These Added?

Google will add automatic extensions based on what it deems appropriate. If your ad is ranked high enough, Google will be more likely to post those extensions, especially if you have a positive rating or lots of good feedback.

These automatic extensions are more likely to show up if you have not added your own extensions in the past.

Opting Out of Ad Extensions

You do not have to have these automatic ad extensions if you don't want them. You can disable these extensions if you feel that they might hurt your listing or if you want to clear some space for some content on your ad listings:

1. Go to the Automated Extension section of the Ads and Extensions section of your site.

2. Review the individual extensions that are showing. The screen should show the total number of impressions that the automatic extensions are producing.

3. Go to the advanced section of the Automated Extension listing.

4. Click that you do not want to have any automated extensions.

   You can select individual automated extensions that you want to stop using. You can allow these to work again later if desired.

5. You can also select to manage automatic call extensions.

   By clicking to stop automatic call extensions, you will state that new extensions will not be created. Any existing extensions you have will still appear. This lets you choose to stop other extensions from showing up and getting in the way of any extensions that you are already working with.

6. Go to the Extensions tab and select the Call Extensions to remove any existing automatic call extensions that you might have added in the past.

Remember that these automatic extensions can help add more content to your listing. The key is to ensure that your content is managed properly and that you have control over what is being included in your listing.

Chapter 26 – Preparing a Call-Only Ad (and Using Forwarding Numbers)

Do you have a phone number that is critical to your business? Your number could be used to let people contact you about delivering or ordering or making appointments.

A Call-Only Ad might be the right thing to use on AdWords. You can create a Call-Only Ad to encourage people to call a specific phone number. You can use this for not only marketing different business features but also encourage mobile users to get in touch with you.

A Call-Only Ad will only work on a device that can make phone calls. This includes mobile devices but also desktop computers that have programs that allow people to click on numbers to call using another app.

The ad will start the call to link someone up to you. You can use any phone number that you want to use including numbers that you might be using in a call extension.

You can also use a forwarding number. This type of number is used to identify how many conversions are being made.

How to Make a Call-Only Ad

You will have to use a few steps to get your Call-Only Ad prepared accordingly:

1. Go to the Ads section of your page on the proper campaign or ad group you want to use.

2. Select the Call-Only Ad option.

3. Select the ad group that your Call-Only Ad will be attached to.

4. Enter the name of your business. This can be up to 25 characters in length.

5. Add the phone number that you want to use.

6. Enter up to two description lines. Each can be up to 80 characters long.

7. Add a display URL to appear at the bottom of the phone listing.

8. Enter a verification URL if desired.

   The verification URL confirms that the phone number your ad is for is linked to the business that holds the number. This ensures that the call will move into the right place.

9. Click to use call reporting and to count conversions as calls from an ad among other things of value. You will be linked to the Conversions menu if you choose to have your content analyzed through something other than your calls.

10. Preview the ad and then Save it.

This does well when linked to the proper keywords in your ad group. Be sure the content of your Call-Only Ad links properly to the rest of your ad.

This process should help you with planning a great Call-Only Ad. The advertisement will be easy to notice and will allow a user to quickly identify what you want to highlight. The user's ability to tap on the ad to call you right away gives you more access to your customers.

Working With a Forwarding Phone Number

While having a Call-Only Ad or call extension will be beneficial, you can make it even better by being able to track your calls. A forwarding phone number will identify when people are reaching your number from your ad. You will have an idea of how well your ads are working when you use a forwarding number.

Someone will click on the Call-Only Ad or call extension that you are using.

Google will forward the call to a temporary number that Google itself has created. The number will lead the user to an AdWords call extension.

The AdWords number will move the call back to the target number the person wants to reach.

The calls that are tracked through the number will be interpreted as conversions.

To include the use of a forwarding phone number:

1. Click to report on the phone call conversions that you get as you set up your Call-Only Ad or call extension.

2. Go to the conversion section of your AdWords account to set up a conversion extension.

3. State that you want your phone calls tracked on the conversion menu.

4. State that you will use the number for calls from a call extension or Call-Only Ad.

5. After creating the conversion data you will use, go to the extension or ad you created earlier and reconfigure its settings to take in the specific ad that you wish to use at a given time.

The process provides you with a way to see if people are calling you from your ads. This works for call-only ads as it gives you an idea of whether or not people are following your ads like you want them to do.

Chapter 27 – Bidding Options and How to Set Values

Now it is time to talk about one of the main points of a Google AdWords listing that will make a difference in how it might be accessed – the bidding process. You will have to place bids on how much you are willing to spend on your ads to have them show up

When you bid to get onto an AdWords search, you will have to look at how you're going to use different options to bid on your searches. You can bid on what you will spend for each click that people put onto your site link, but there are many options outside of that to choose from.

You will have to look at how you are bidding on keywords so you have more control over how well your ads can appear on a search.

This chapter also includes what you can do when getting your bids set up. You will have the option to prepare a daily budget to decide the maximum amount of money you will spend per click.

CPC – Cost Per Click

The basic bidding option you can work with on AdWords is the CPC or Cost Per Click option where you will pay each time someone clicks on an ad. This works for when you are trying to draw demand for your product or service.

The CPC is perfect for when you are aiming to get people to visit your website. You can use this when you need to get people to learn about your site or to get on a page to see what you have for sale.

CPM – Cost Per Impression

You don't necessarily have to work with the CPC bidding standard to get on Google AdWords. You can use the CPM or CPA method.

The CPM refers to the Cost Per Impression. You can specify that you want to bid on it based on the number of impressions you will reach.

The CPM is typically measured by the thousands. That is, you can spend a certain amount of money for 1,000 impressions. You can use this to help you get more people to notice your site.

To set up the CPM:

1. You will have to prepare the CPM total when you create a new campaign.

2. Click on the Campaigns button and then select the option to start a new campaign.

3. Enter the details surrounding your campaign.

4. While in the campaign settings section, select the CPM bid strategy.

5. Decide how much you will spend on those impressions at a time.

6. Continue with creating the campaign.

You can always adjust the total bid later, which will be discussed in another section.

CPA - Cost Per Acquisition

The CPA measurement refers to the Cost Per Acquisition. You can use this to focus on when people are going to click on specific things on your site or when those people might enter something else on your site. This is more specific in nature than other options.

You would have to set up this option when you create a campaign. The instructions for doing so are the same as with other options. Make sure you decide on the parameters associated with the acquisition.

You can list information on the acquisition such as a sale of a certain product, or someone signing up for an email newsletter and so forth.

You will also have to set up the conversion tracking process on your AdWords site. Details on this will be covered later. Conversion tracking ensures that certain bits of content are shared at a time.

How to Set a Bid Value

To set up a CPC bid or any other bid type:

1. Go to the page for your campaign or ad group.

2. Click on the campaign or group that you wish to adjust the bid.

   The page should include information on what your maximum bid is. This is based on your daily budget and what you plan on spending on each click. The bid information will be adjusted based on many parameters that were created when you started your ad.

3. After clicking on an option, choose the Change Maximum CPC (or another style) Bids option.

The page should list information on what you can do. You can choose to set a new bid total or to increase or decrease your bid by a certain percentage. You can also raise the value of your bids to get on the first page of Google's search results, but this might require you to spend a little extra money to make this possible.

This strategy lets you do this with as many campaigns or ad groups as you wish. You can adjust the values one at a time or you can click on multiple groups or features to adjust their values to be the same for all.

Changing a Bid Strategy

You have the option to change your bid strategy at any point. You can change a CPC to CPN bid style, for instance. You have to adjust the individual keywords that you are targeting.

This process allows you to use many strategies within a campaign or ad group. Certain keywords will concentrate on one strategy while others will use something else. The keywords section of your AdWords dashboard allows you to see how your content is organized.

1. Go to the Campaigns section of the site.

2. Click on the Keywords section.This will reveal details on all the keywords used throughout your campaigns.

3. Select the keywords you want to utilize for your change.

4. Click the Edit button and select the option to change the bids, the bid strategy you want to use, or other parameters.

5. Select the type of bidding option you wish to use.

The convenient thing about this is that you can use this when you notice certain keywords that might not be prominent. For instance, you can have keywords that do not appear often to be charged by the click. Keywords that appear more often can be charged by the number of impressions being produced.

Planning Bid Adjustments

Another feature you can use involves using different bid adjustments. An adjustment allows you to show your ads more or less often based on many factors:

- The device is used when making a search. You might pay more for a click on a search made on a desktop computer and less for a search on a tablet, for instance. This is when you notice that people are more likely to reach you from certain sources or devices.

- A person's location. This is a campaign-level adjustment that lets you bid more to reach people located in certain places.

- Ad schedules. This is another campaign-level parameter. This is when you want to pay more to get online at a specific time.

- Target audiences. Designed with certain ad groups in mind, this is when you have very specific audiences that you want to reach.

  This is perfect for when you have certain things that you want to promote to specific groups of people. Even better, this helps you to plan a better strategy for managing your bids. With this, you can easily create a new campaign that fits your budget. You will not have to spend too much on clicks that might not come as often, but you will also direct your plans toward ads that are going to be more worthwhile and may be easier for people to click on.

To plan a bid adjustment:

1. Click on the locations, ad schedule, or any other parameter that you want to use to make your bid adjustment.

   Do this within the campaign or ad group that you want to create the adjustment. Remember that the rules for doing so are varied based on the type of project that you wish to use in any situation.

2. Select the campaign or ad group for which you want to make a bid adjustment.

3. Select a row that you wish to adjust.

4. Enter details on how much of a change in your bid adjustment.

   In most cases, you will have to adjust the bid based on a certain percentage. Be ready to decide on an appropriate total for this based on what you wish to attain from your project.

5. Click to Save the total change that you wish to make.

This process should be simple to ensure that your bids are arranged properly and that you have a good plan for making your work stand out and be more dynamic.

Excluding An Ad From a Specific Parameter

A related strategy you can use for getting your bids managed is excluding your ads from a certain parameter. In this situation, you can delete your ad from a specific time, device, or another parameter by decreasing the bid by 100 percent. This keeps your ad from being visible in situations where you do not want it to appear.

Working with the bids that you can use for your AdWords campaign is important, but it is a necessity to look at how your campaign is laid out based on how you will market your work.

Chapter 28 – How Are the Order and Cost Determined?

The interesting thing about working with AdWords is that you will not list a specific amount of money that you want to spend on a bid, but you can use a daily budget.

You might assume that those who pay the most money to use Google AdWords will be more likely to show up at the top of the listing. The truth about AdWords is that it requires more than just money. You have to create a quality advertisement that is intriguing to the reader while also favored by Google.

A unique process is used to decide the order of the results that will appear on a search. Google considers all the websites that are linked to a keyword and will analyze their links and the amounts of money they are spending to determine which ones are the best. It is all about the quality of the link and not so much about the money being spent.

The best way to explain the process is that it is like an auction. During the auction, advertisers will find the keywords that they want to use in their advertisements. They will determine how much money they will spend on them as well.

The auction process not only determines which ads will show up but also what is going to be spent. The good news is that you will never pay more than the maximum amount that you have determined you can handle at a time, but you must still be aware of how your cost per click will surely change.

As you will notice through this process, it will be important to create a better advertisement while using a good landing page. This is to make it easier for your ad to be visible but also to reduce the total amount of money you would spend on an ad.

You need to use the right plan so you can make your content easy to spot while getting more people involved before you have spent your daily maximum amount.

Getting the Auction Ready

The order in which the ads will appear will be determined not long after a user enters in a keyword. When a person enters a keyword into the search box, Google will review the AdWords entries that are linked to that specific keyword. There must be enough entries for Google to decide to have an auction.

The specific number that Google uses is unclear, but you will certainly notice when there are two or three ads on a search that there is a significantly larger number of people to have the auction.

There is a limit as to how many times a single group can enter an auction. A single advertiser will only be able to have one entry for the auction. The advertiser will have to choose the proper ad copy and other details to ensure that it can enter the auction.

The Value of the Quality Score

To make this work, the advertisers have to follow Google's Quality Score index. This plays a vital role in determining which ads are going to be listed first. The Quality Score is a measurement on a scale of 1 to 10 of how effective a site is. When the score is higher, the ad is more relevant and useful.

The Quality Score will be discussed in a separate chapter later in this guide. The score is very detailed as it is based on many factors, but it works mainly with quality and relevance as well as how many people might interact with the ad at a time.

Determining the Ad Rank

Google analyzes all ads linked to a keyword based on the money being offered and other factors that relate to the Quality Score.

The ad rank is the product of a simple equation.

1. The maximum bid total that one is aiming to spend will be calculated. This refers to how much someone is willing to spend for each click.

2. The Quality Score is then tallied. The score is multiplied by the maximum bid.

3. This produces the overall ad rank. The entry that has the largest ad rank will be the first one to appear on the search result.

4. The second and third-highest ad ranks (if applicable) will appear at the top of the search below the first one.

Here's an example of how this works. Let's say that you have an ad with a Quality Score of 6. Meanwhile, you are willing to spend $3 as your maximum bid. Your ad rank would be 18 at this point.

There might be a competitor with a Quality Score of 8 and is willing to spend $1.50 per click. That person's ad rank will only be 12. Therefore, your ad will appear on the search first because you are paying more money even though the Quality Score is not as high.

But at the same time, a person with a Quality Score of 3 might be willing to spend $5 per click. That person has an ad rank of 15, thus meaning that the person is going to show up but will have a high premium.

The point is simple – you need a better Quality Score to show up on the listing without having to spend too much money. Those whose links are not of the best quality will have to spend more money just to get online, although they can always use other measures to help them make their links more attractive.

How Much Will You Spend Per Click?

You are not necessarily going to pay the maximum amount. You will pay a certain total that is based on the results of the auction. Your charge will be based on a CPC or cost per click basis.

1. The ad rank of the entity that is directly below you will be factored in at the start.

2. That ad rank is divided by your Quality Score.

3. Add 1 cent to the total to figure out the actual CPC that you will spend.

Let's go back to the example where your Quality Score is 6 and you will spend up to $3 per click. Now think about that group that had an ad rank of 15. At this point, you would divide 15 by 6 to get 2.5. Add a cent to this to get a total of $2.51 per click.

That group with the rank of 15 and a quality of 3 would be listed above a group with a rank of 12. Take 12 and divide it by 3 to get a CPC of $4.01. This is still below the maximum of $5 that the party is willing to spend, but still be a higher total due to the lower Quality Score.

What if the CPC that comes about is higher than the maximum bid total? In that case, a site would not be able to get online because it is not spending enough. The entry would have to either spend extra or improve the score by changing the link. Refer to the Quality Score chapter to see more about this point.

Similar rules are used for the other bidding options that can be chosen. Experiment with different bidding choices when deciding what you can do with your campaign to make it stronger and more dynamic.

Chapter 29 – The Quality Score and How to Improve It

To get the most out of your Google AdWords listing, you will have to produce something that has a better Quality Score. This will determine how well your listing will be highlighted in a Google search. The sites that have the largest Quality Scores will be more likely to appear at the top of an AdWords listing.

The Quality Score is a measure of two things:

1. The relevance of the keyword, advertisement, and URL

2. The user's experience

When the two points are combined together, it becomes easier for a good Quality Score to be calculated. The best part is that you can regularly check your score yourself. This allows you to make regular adjustments to your ads and landing pages so you can get a better score. This in turn not only makes you get your ad to show up but also possibly lowers the cost associated with each click. This increases the profits that you might get provided that people purchase more items after getting onto your site through the ads you are posting.

How Google Reviews Your Quality Score

When reviewing your site to decide your Quality Score, Google uses the following steps:

1. The click-through rate on your site will be analyzed at the beginning.

   The click-through rate or CTR is a measurement of how many times people click on a link based on the number of impressions it gets. A site with a better CTR is one that gets more people to click on it.

The CTR can be found by dividing the total number of clicks on an ad by the number of impressions. Naturally, there are going to be people who will not click on the ad even after it was exposed. The CTR is a necessary measurement as it reviews how well a site's ads are working and if people are actually finding the site.

2. The keyword being used must be relevant to the advertisement being produced.

   For instance, a local ice cream parlor would have to create enough words and features in its listing showing that it is devoted to selling ice cream. When the link has enough content relating to ice cream, that ad will become more popular.

3. The quality of the landing page is checked alongside the relevance of the subject.

   The landing page should be easy to read and load up. It must include content that relates to the keyword being used.

4. The ad text must also be relevant.

   The ad text has to include enough terms and features.

5. Even the historical AdWords performance that someone has had in the past may be incorporated into the process.

Although this last part might seem daunting for people who have just started to use AdWords, this is not necessarily something that a person has to be worried about. Besides,

Google has not revealed information on how it favors those five factors.

You will have to watch for how the Quality Score on your link is produced. When the score is higher, you will have a better chance of getting your Google AdWords link to have a higher score.

How the is Score Measured

Your Google AdWords link will be measured on a scale of 1 to 10. You can find your score by doing the following:

1. Go to the campaign you are trying to review in your AdWords account.

2. Click on the Customize Columns section on the group table.

3. Choose to see the Quality Score.

4. You should now see the Quality Score for each keyword you are using.

The scores are listed from 1 to 10 with 10 being the best possible score and 5 is considered to be the main benchmark by Google.

Google will charge you less per click when you have a higher score. A score of 10 will result in you paying 50 percent less than the standard cost for a click. Of course, the base value will vary based on the keyword you are using. The highest score will get the biggest discount as the ad will be determined to be the one that has the best possible value attached to it.

You will pay much more for a click if you have a weaker link. A site with a score of 1 will pay 400 percent the base value for a click. A score of 2 will have an increase of 150 percent and a score of 3 has a 67.3 percent added charge.

Google uses these added charges to ensure that only the best possible links appear. This does not mean that a weaker link cannot appear, but it will cost more to have the link work.

For Google, each advertisement is about quality over quantity. Anyone who wants to get an ad ready but doesn't focus on the quality of the ad content will have to spend more money on it.

Steps to Increase Your Quality Score

You must get your Quality Score if you want your link to appear online while having a cheaper cost per click. Fortunately, there are several steps you can use to help you get your Quality Score to increase:

1. Find new keywords that are relevant to your campaign. Add those new keywords to your site. These new keywords can include long-tail keywords that are very specific to whatever you are selling. These long-tail keywords will be responsible for a large portion of your web traffic.

2. Get your keywords organized into a series of groups. Keep the keywords split up so they only appear in groups where those words would surely be relevant.

3. Review your ad text and adjust it as needed. You might have to change your ad text to be more specific and relate directly to a very particular subsection of your audience.

4. Check the landing pages that your sites are linked to. Adjust those pages to better fit in with your campaigns. Do not assume that Google is not going to pay attention

to the sites and information to which your links are connected. Google will analyze everything you are using in your campaign. Make sure you create a good landing page that focuses on the keywords you are using while being as specific as possible.

5. Review the negative keywords that are bogging down your progress. Take a look at the keywords you are using. Are there any keywords that are there for no reason? Maybe there are irrelevant keywords that are not related to your page.

Check your Quality Score regularly to see how well your campaign is running so you can identify what you can do to improve your score.

Chapter 30 – Conversion Tracking

The conversions that you get from AdWords should be analyzed based on your messages. AdWords can assist you with tracking how your conversions are developing. You can see which keywords, ad groups, and other things drive customers to take action and interact with you. The information you get from tracking will help you to make the right choices about how your content is used and what people will see.

Conversion tracking is a solution to identify how your ad clicks are working. It measures when people get onto your site and use it. With conversion tracking, you will get information on what people are doing on your site.

The tracking process is vital for CPA campaigns and ad groups. When the right tracking plans are used, it becomes easier for AdWords to charge you based on the amount of money you are putting into your ads.

How Tracking Works

Conversion tracking is about more than just seeing when people click on your ads. It is also about what happens after a person clicks on your ad.

What will someone do after getting to your site from the ad you created? Is that person going to download a file? Will that person sign up for email newsletters or buy something you are offering? The conversion tracking feature lets you know what people are doing after they get to your site.

Tracking works with a simple setup:

1. You will trigger a conversion action on your account. You will set up a profile based on something that people could do.

2. A tag or other bit of content is then installed on your site.

3. You will then get information on the Conversions menu of AdWords about how often people click on a link and when they get to certain sections.

Accessing the Conversion Menu

To get the conversion menu to work for you:

1. Go to the Tools section listed by the wrench on the top right part of your site.

2. Select the Conversions option.

3. Click on the +Conversion button to get started.

At this point, you will have many options to work with for your conversions. You can use as many conversions as needed, but you should look at the situation surrounding your ad campaign to give you more control.

What the Page Reviews

The page should give you information on everything relating to how often things are being counted, the types of conversions you are reviewing and so forth.

You can also get information on three things relating to the content you are using:

1. All Conversions - This includes details on the number of conversions that have been produced.

2. Repeat Rate - The repeat rate lists the number of conversions that were sent out based on interactions that produced one or more conversions.

3. All Conversion Value - Tracks information on each conversion action that is being supported.

These three sections and many others identify everything working on your site. You can use the Analytics featured on the Conversion page to get an idea of how each of the conversions you are using is working.

Tracking Website Conversions

The first part of conversion tracking to use is reviewing website conversions.

1. Enter a conversion name. This can be up to 100 characters in length.

2. Select the category that you wish to track.

   You can choose to track one of the following qualities:

   • Review how many times people make purchases after reaching your site through an AdWords link.

   • Get details on sign-ups. This includes data on how people are signing up for an email newsletter to learn more about you or your site.

   • Review the leads that people are getting from your site.

   • The number of views of a key page.

   • You can also use another option by selecting the Other choice.

You should look at how different qualities might appear on your site above others. Look at what you are using here so you have more control.

3. Select the value of whatever you are going to use.

   You can use the same value for each conversion you produce or different values for each one. You can also avoid using a value. The value setting lets you see what makes certain conversions more valuable or appropriate to use.

   When a conversion takes place, AdWords will record the value and use this value as the conversion total. This shows what you are spending at a given time. You should see how the values of different purchases or actions might vary based on what you are using with AdWords.

4. Choose the number of conversions that you will count for each click.

   AdWords can choose to review every conversion or you can focus on only one conversion at a time so you can get a clear idea of specific things that trigger people to make particular moves on your site.

   For instance, you can choose AdWords to count every conversion. This means that when someone makes three orders on your site, you will get three conversions listed. By using the option to track just one click or action, those three orders will be just one conversion according to the program.

5. Enter some dates relating to when you want to get the conversions reported.

6. After you continue to the next menu, you will get information on what you can do next.

7. Choose to either use Google Tag Manager or install the tag on your own.

   When you choose to install your own tag, you will get an HTML code that will be added somewhere on your site. You can start by creating a tag that brings visitors to a marketing list you are running. You can also use Google Tag Manager to install a tracking tag if you prefer.

Adding a Conversion Tracking Tag

Your conversion tracking tag is vital to the success of your AdWords campaign. You will use this to know how often people are getting to your site and interacting with it.

1. Make sure the conversion action on your AdWords account is active.

   You can download the tracking snippet that you generated as you created the conversion tracking tag initially.

2. See that you can also edit your website. You must have the ability to do this to get more out of your campaign.

3. Find a conversion page on your site.

   You can select a page that thanks a person for signing up for emails or for making a purchase. A page may also include a very specific part of your site.

4. Go to the head tags on your HTML code.

5. Paste the tag in between the head tags. Start with the global site tag and then work with any event snippets you will add.

6. Save the changes to your site.

At this point, your tag should start working. You can review AdWords regularly to see how well the content is being managed.

Using the Google Tag Manager

It might be easier for you to get tags ready when you use the Google Tag Manager. This setup simplifies the approach associated with creating tags for conversions.

To use Google Tag Manager, you will need to sign up for the service. This can be done for free at the Google Analytics website.

1. Go to the Conversions section of your AdWords account.

2. Click on the specific conversion that you want to review or get one ready yourself.

3. When setting up the tag, click to use Google Tag Manager. You can also do this with an existing conversion by clicking on the proper box next to it and selecting the option from the menu to use the Tag Manager program.

4. Collect the Conversion ID for your tag and the conversion label that will be used for your specific conversion event. Google automatically produces these two markers to make your conversion tag distinguishable.

5. Go to the Google Tag Manager program.

6. Enter the ID and label being used in the proper section of your site.

7. Go to the Triggering section and enter details on what tag should be recorded. The triggers should be whatever it is you want to get out of the conversion.

8. Click the Save button.

9. You can use the Tag Manager program to simulate how well the triggering function works. A test can be used to see if the action that you want to record is actually being recorded based on the tags or events you are listing.

The process takes a bit of time, but it helps you to get all your tags ready and easy to analyze. Be sure you see how this works when determining what will make your content attractive.

Tracking App Conversions

The next set of conversions to review involves the cases where people install apps or complete in-app actions. You can use one of three solutions for tracking apps conversions.

With AdWords, you can review when people install apps. You can use this by tracking the number of downloads from Google Play, Firebase, or some third-party program. By using this, you will know if people are responding to any promotions you have by downloading an app you might have to offer. This gives you an idea of what ads are the most effective for marketing your app.

More importantly, this review shows how well your ads are working based on their values. When you get information on what people are spending on your apps from certain ads, you will see if certain ads are worthwhile.

Using Firebase

The first option you have for tracking app conversions is to use Firebase. This is a mobile development platform that has been popular as a solution for managing quality apps. The platform has been in operation since 2011, but it has become even more prominent since 2014 when Google acquired it.

1. Start by getting a Firebase account ready. You will need a Firebase project that you can link up to your AdWords account.

2. Enter details on conversion events in your Firebase program.

   You can use up to ten conversion events on your applications with Firebase. Make sure you use the Firebase program to adjust the conversion parameters that you wish to use.

3. Link Firebase to your AdWords account. Go to the Linked Accounts section of Firebase and then select the specific Firebase account you have.

   You must make sure the Firebase account you have is active and that you are properly logged onto it. Also, your Firebase account administrator should identify you as the owner of the account before it will work for you.

4. Go to the Conversions section of your AdWords account and then select to review conversions for apps. Enter the choice of using Firebase.

5. You should notice the Firebase events that you have produced.

   You might have to check the Linked Accounts section of your account to see if you have your Firebase account linked.

6. Click the checkboxes for each individual event that you wish to address.

7. Enter a value for each conversion that you will use. You can assign values based on things like when people install apps or when they open them.

8. Adjust the conversion window within the settings for the conversion.

   This refers to the amount of time that a conversion is to be included. You might consider events that happen a week after someone downloads an app to count as conversions.

Using Firebase helps you know the results of the mobile conversions.

Tracking With Google Play

Google Play is a popular marketplace for Android apps. You can use it to get information on what people are doing when designing your apps.

1. Link your Google Play account to AdWords. Go to the Linked Accounts section and click on Google Play.

2. Enter the email address of the Google Play account holder.

3. Have the account holder to approve the request.

   The best thing to do is to use an email that you control yourself. If you are going to ask someone else to approve the request, you must discuss your plans with that person ahead of time. Remember that your AdWords account will not adjust anything on the Google Play account and vice versa.

4. After the accounts are linked, choose to monitor installs.

5. Enter the specific name of the app you are targeting. Remember that this is only for Android apps.

6. Select a value for each action that you are tracking. The value should be the price of the app being downloaded.

7. Click the box to include your conversions into your AdWords reports.

   This is to get information on how many people are downloading your apps and what you are earning from them. This information on what you are earning can be compared to the average value of the costs per click that lead to the application downloads.

You can also choose to track in-app purchases with these steps:

1. When using the setup, select the In-App Purchase option instead of the Installs choice at the beginning.

2. Enter the app you are going to track.

3. Select if you will track every conversion per ad click or just one per click.

Using the option to track every ad is best as there is a chance people will make more than one in-app purchase on a program.

4. Click on the conversion window option to see how long the window for conversions after a purchase or download takes place.

The convenient thing about using Google Play is that, like Firebase, the program will reveal how people use your app after arriving at a certain link.

Using a Third-Party Program

You can use one of many third-party programs to track your conversions.

1. Get your AdWords account linked to the third-party program you've chosen.

   Earlier in this guide, there are instructions to get a third-party tracking program linked to your account. Third-party programs are all different.

2. Select the Third-Party App Analytics option on the conversions menu.

3. Check on the individual Analytics events that are linked to your third-party program.

   Double-check to see what is linked to your site and that it is working properly.

4. After choosing individual options, set the values and conversion windows for each. Click to import each of these and then continue.

After you do this, you will get new conversion data to work with.

Tracking Phone Calls

One of the best things about mobile ads on AdWords is that you can get your phone number listed on an appropriate extension or on your main page so a mobile user can tap on it to directly get in touch. You have to do this before you can work with this option in the conversions section.

Calls From Call Extensions or Call-Only Ads

There are three options when tracking phone calls. First, you can review calls from the extensions that you use or also from the call-only ads that you have created.

1. Create a proper ad in one of these two forms.

2. State that you want to use call tracking for each of these ads.

3. Go to the conversion menu and then select to track phone calls followed by stating that you are ready to review content from your extension or Call-Only Ad.

4. Enter details on the conversion name.

5. List the type of conversion action you are tracking - basic information is the best.

6. List details on the value of each phone call. Don't assign a value to a call if you are not interested in this.

7. Enter the number of conversions to count for each call. Use just one conversion for each call from your ad.

   List the minimum length for a call before it can count as a conversion - 30 to 60 seconds in most cases.

8. Confirm the conversion that you wish to use.

This will work with the ads or extensions that you are willing to track.

Tracking Calls via a Phone Number on Your Website

You can also track calls that from a phone number that you have posted on your website. This can be used if you have a forwarding number linked to your account.

1. Get a call extension ready.

2. Set up space on your website where you can enter a conversion tracking code.

3. Go to the Conversions menu, select the option to have your conversion track back to a number on your website.

4. Enter the type of category for your conversion.

5. List the value and count of your calls.

6. Enter information at the bottom including how long a call has to be for it to count as a conversion in seconds and the conversion window you will use in days.

7. After you click the Create and Continue button, you will be given a tag.

8. Select whether you have installed a global tag on your site.

   You can use a tag from another Google product. If you do not have it, you can get AdWords to create the full tag that you would add to your site. You also have the option to modify the tag, but this requires a good deal of technical knowledge.

9. After this, you can install the tag yourself. Copy the tag and paste is between the head tags on each page of your site that shows your number.

10. You can also use the Google Tag Manager if you have a website supported by Google. This will let you upload codes to your site and Google will analyze the content. This is useful if you do not have much technical knowledge of how to code a site.

11. A phone snippet must also be added to each page that has your phone number. This will link your phone number to the Google forwarding number you are using.

    Be sure the content is added to the code for each page. The AdWords website can walk you through the technical process to have the content linked properly.

Tracking Clicks on Your Number Through Your Mobile Site

The mobile version of your website can also include information on your phone number. A person can tap on that number or type in the number into their mobile device shortly after visiting your site.

You do not need to get a Google forwarding number to make this option work, but you will still need to add a tag.

1. Click on the option in the Conversions menu to track clicks on a number that comes via a mobile site.

2. Enter all the details on the sections as listed earlier. These include the sections for counting conversions

and their values as well as timing for calls to be conversions.

3. Select whether you want to use Google Tag Manager or if you want to install your tags yourself.

4. You should get both a global site tag and an event snippet to use throughout your mobile site.

5. Review the AdWords website for specifics on where to get the code added. The tags should go along the head tags on each page on your mobile site.

By using these steps, you can get detailed information on how well your calls are being tracked and tagged.

Importing Conversions from Other Sources

You can also work with other sources to prepare your conversion data. The process has many extra options, but you should use the appropriate instructions:

1. Click on the Import option when preparing your conversions.

2. Select the program that you will use to import your content.

   You can work with Google Analytics, Firebase, Salesforce, or other programs.

3. Link the proper account of one of these programs to AdWords.

4. Click on the proper events that you want to use.

The process for doing this will vary based on the program you are using. You can review the individual sections of this book for details on using Firebase, Google Analytics, or Salesforce. For other third-party programs, the rules will vary.

You will find it is not too hard to make the most of AdWords.

Obtaining Consent

Although these options to obtain information on other people through AdWords can be convenient, you must make sure you get the consent of the people that you are targeting for this the information.

To obtain consent:

1. Enter details on the bottom part of your site that lists information on any data that you might collect.

2. Make sure you mention that the data you are gathering does not include any identifiable data relating to individual users.

3. You should also discuss details on any cookies or other tracking programs that are used to track users who visit a site. Again, this content should not be anything that immediately identifies someone.

This part of getting conversions tracked is needed to let people know what you are collecting and that you will use the data responsibly.

Chapter 31 – Policies for the Use of Keywords and Ad Content

The beauty of Google AdWords is that it supports advertisements for products and services of all kinds. However, that does not mean that every single thing that people submit to AdWords will be accepted or considered for marketing purposes.

When you look at the keywords on your AdWords page, you will notice a listing that says "Policy details." This includes details on any keywords that have been approved by AdWords for your use as well as ones that are eligible. You may even notice that some of your keywords were not approved.

So, why would any keywords you want to use on AdWords be rejected? The reason is there are many policies that Google uses that relate to how your content is presented.

Your keywords, your ad content and even your landing page might be deemed to be inappropriate for AdWords. Google will review your content to determine if you will be allowed to use AdWords.

Google has some very specific parameters that you must follow if you want to get your content listed online. Not following the rules will keep your campaign from running like you want.

Eligible Keywords and Ads

Some keywords or ads in your campaign might be listed as eligible. These are keywords and ads that are being reviewed by Google can still be used on your AdWords campaign.

An eligible keyword is one that Google needs to take a closer look at before approving. Google will determine if a keyword is usable or if there is a problem with it. For instance, you might notice that the keyword "vacuum cleaners for sale" has been accepted but "Rug Doctor vacuum cleaners for sale" is eligible. This is because Google needs to look at the ad to see that you are genuinely providing people with vacuums from that brand.

Meanwhile, an ad will be identified based on the keywords used. Sometimes an ad will include a brand name or some other words that relate to an industry that Google might not like.

An eligible ad will have to be reviewed by Google before it can be accepted. This will only take one business day in most cases. It might take longer depending on the specific features of the ad.

An eligible ad and keyword can still run on AdWords even before the content is approved. However, that ad will not be shown to people who have the SafeSearch filtering program turned on. SafeSearch is designed to prevent people from seeing ads designed specifically with adult content in mind. These include ads with sexual content, unusual financial schemes or anything involving weapons or other items marketed for self-protection. Most people who use Google have SafeSearch turned on, thus dramatically reducing the number of people that can see your ad.

Also, Google will not let eligible ads appear on the Display Network or through any search partners. Google has to review and approve everything before those ads can be seen on those pages. This also reduces the reach of your ads. You will have to wait to get the problem resolved before your ads can appear online.

The worst thing about your content being eligible is that it might be innocent and simple in nature. At the same time, your ad will be restricted as to how it might appear. Your ad may appear, but that does not mean Google will actually highlight the ad to your satisfaction.

How to Dispute An Eligible Keyword

You might have a great keyword and notice it is being questioned by Google. Maybe you are selling a guidebook that will help people to quit smoking tobacco. You might see that the keyword is listed as questionable because it includes the word "tobacco." This is in spite of how you are not selling tobacco but rather a product to help people with quitting their tobacco habit.

When you have a keyword that you are trying to confirm but Google is holding you up, you have the option to have it disputed. When you do this, you are letting Google know that you have a keyword that needs to be confirmed. You will tell Google that you need to get this keyword approved as soon as possible so you can get your ad running.

You should get an answer in one business day as to whether your eligible keyword will be accepted. Sometimes it might take a little longer. This is due to the ad being a little more detailed or complicated or maybe because the keyword is lengthy. Perhaps there is a deeper context involved with the keyword that you are trying to use. You might have a keyword like "quit tobacco book," but Google might question its context. With the right process, Google will eventually notice that whatever you are promoting has a sensible context to it.

To dispute an issue:

1.   Go to the Google AdWords Help Desk.

To specifically dispute an eligible keyword, use the URL https://support.google.com/adwords/contact/approval _request.

2. Enter your name, contact email, and AdWords customer ID.

3. Select the language of your ad.

4. List the topic of the ad. The choices include traditional retail as well as sections relating to alcohol, gambling, healthcare, financial services, and weapons.

5. Click on what you want to review - either an ad, keyword, or extension.

6. List details on the issue with your content.

   Be as specific as possible. Let Google know about the concern you have and what you want to do. Be ready to spend some time having your content reviewed and confirmed. It might take a few business days for Google to complete its review.

Prohibited Industries on AdWords

Regardless of the keywords you are using and the ads you write, you must be fully aware of what you are putting on AdWords. Google might penalize you or delete you altogether if you engage in certain prohibited actions.

Google has several standards for what you can and cannot do online. These standards focus on products that might be dangerous or risky to promote. You must be aware of some of the industries that are prohibited on AdWords:

1. Counterfeit Products

   Counterfeit items are products that contain trademarks, logos, and other identifying marks that make a product look like something from another brand. For instance, a counterfeit Michael Kors handbag might come with a color or pattern similar to what the designer accessory company uses. A counterfeiter might have copied the design and even included the same Michael Kors logo imprint of the genuine handbag. This could be sold to people at a very cheap rate.

   In reality, this is an illegal practice. While it is fine to produce a handbag that is somewhat inspired by what a high-end company has made, it is outright illegal to make it look exactly like the original product including identifying labels and other features. Google does not allow people to advertise counterfeit goods on AdWords.

2. Dangerous Products

   Google wants to ensure that people are protected when finding products for sale. As a result, Google will not allow people to market potentially dangerous products. Anything that can cause injury or be threatening to others will not be accepted by AdWords.

   Some of the dangerous products that Google does not support on AdWords include:

   - Recreational drugs; this is regardless of whether they are herbal or chemical

   - Any materials used to facilitate the use of said drugs

- Computer hacking materials

- Weapons, including handguns

- Ammunition for such weapons

- Any explosive materials, including fireworks

- Instructions for making explosive items or weapons

- Tobacco products

Any keywords or ads that relate to these illegal activities will be outlawed altogether. Be sure your keywords and ad copy do not reference any of these items. Even a casual reference to fireworks might be frowned upon because it could take some time for Google to notice you are not actually trying to sell them. You might say "See the fireworks fly when you lose weight today!" but that might be rejected because the word "fireworks" is included. You have to submit your issue to Google and wait for it to be accepted and approved. Avoiding references to anything that is outlawed is the best practice.

3. Anything That Encourages Dishonest Behavior

Google believes that people need to be honest and direct with others. Those who encourage people to be dishonest or cut corners are not welcome on AdWords. Some of the behaviors that encourage dishonesty that Google has outlawed include:

- Hacking programs

- Anything that artificially inflates traffic or usage on your site

- Fake documents, including false diplomas or user identification cards

- Academic cheating services, including services that provide someone to write a paper for you or to take a test for you

You need to avoid making direct or even indirect references to these items. Even using the term "life hack" might be risky even if you are being innocent and just want people to see what is available.

4. Content That Is Generally Inappropriate Or Hostile

AdWords has disallowed anything hateful and hostile, aims to intimidate, offensive or dangerous to others. This includes such content as:

- Bullying behaviors or any other form of intimidation; this includes bullying specific people or certain subsections based on nationality, race, gender, sexual orientation and so forth

- Hate group contents, this including current and historic documents

- Graphic images, including crime scene or autopsy images

- Content relating to abusing others, including animal, child, elder abuse and abuse to the disabled

- Content involving violent behaviors, including murder or self-harm

- Extortion or blackmail data

- The sale of items relating to endangered animals, including the sale of ivory, pelts, and meat from such animals

- Any content that uses profanity

  In other words, be nice to people and avoid being rude. Even if you are using profanity as a joke, you should still avoid it altogether. The odds are some people might understand that you are joking.

If whatever you are promoting sounds like it is going to hurt people in any way, it will more than likely be rejected. Check your keywords and ad copy just to be safe. Of course, you should always use your common sense. If it is offensive to people or possibly illegal to sell, you should probably refrain from marketing it.

Limited Industries on AdWords

Some industries can still be promoted on AdWords, but they can only be highlighted on a limited basis. There are two reasons why you might not be fully able to promote certain items on Facebook:

1. You might be promoting something that is not available to people in all age groups. This includes alcoholic products that are not available to those under 21 years of age.

2. Your content might also be culturally sensitive to some people. Gambling activities might be prohibited in certain countries or by those who have specific religious values.

You can still promote content relating to any of these industries on AdWords. However, you would have to go through an extensive process to get your content approved. Also, your content will not be shown in every location nor will it be accessible to every person based on age and other demographics.

Some products you may want to sell aren't appropriate for everyone. You obviously cannot get wine accessories sold to people 21 years of age or younger. At the same time, there's a chance you won't be able to sell those things in some places because the expenses might be too high.

The following industries are interpreted by Google AdWords are being limited industries. They are self-explanatory for the most part, but you should know how the keywords you use will relate closely to some of these fields:

1. Adult Content

   Adult content refers to marketing for gentleman's clubs, adult magazines, and videos, sex toys, or sites that offer photos of naked people or those in sexual positions. Matchmaking sites are also interpreted as adult content as sometimes these sites entail people looking for specific sexual encounters. Sexual enhancement products are also restricted.

   Adult content will only show up on searches for people who are old enough to use such services. This content may also be limited as to geographic location and the rules involved with using services in certain areas.

2. Alcohol

   Advertising any kind of alcoholic product will be restricted on AdWords. This is due to limits on who can consume alcohol, but also places do not allow advertising alcoholic products in any form. Also, there are rules over where such products can be mailed as well.

Even non-alcoholic versions of alcoholic products are restricted on AdWords including non-alcoholic beer products.

3. Gambling Activities

Gambling activities are restricted due to age limits of who can gamble and rules on advertising. Your ads might not appear in regions where advertising for gaming activities is illegal or limited. Such gambling activities that are prohibited by AdWords include:

- Promoting physical casinos

- Highlighting online casinos

- Online sportsbooks, poker rooms or other places that offer gambling content

- Places that teach people how to gamble

Places that offer promo codes for gambling sites but do not actually offer gambling activities are restricted by AdWords. Those sites are still encouraging people to engage in gambling.

Some places might be less restrictive than others. Online betting can be promoted in the United Kingdom and also Canada to a lesser extent, but the same cannot be said for the United States.

4. Copyrights

   Copyrights are heavily restricted on AdWords. You would have to get certification to offer something that has been copyrighted on AdWords. The next chapter includes details on how you can attain this certification.

5. Health Care Services

   Health care service sites that offer information on healthy routines and medicines can be restricted by Google. This is because some sites are known to engage in questionable actions and not likely to offer useful information. You must review the regulations for any areas that you want to target to see what you can and cannot promote.

6. Political Content

   Political content has to be reviewed carefully. Any political ads to be posted on AdWords would have to follow the appropriate campaign and election laws in the particular areas. Ads would need to be suspended during certain time periods when political advertising is not allowed.

   Political content includes content that focuses on a certain political candidate or party that is running for election. Any sites that focus on a certain partisan political issue will be restricted as well. Such restrictions are used to keep the arena of political discourse fair while also preventing people from trying to convey harmful or false information to others.

7. Trademarks

   Trademarks might be used in some advertisements. These include trademarks of products from a specific brand name you are marketing. You will have to remove ads if you did not get the approval to use the trademark or you are using that trademark with harmful intentions in mind. A trademark holder has the right to submit a complaint to Google if it believes an ad using its trademark is inappropriate or misleading.

8. Financial Services

   Financial services are restricted by age and location due to the types of services people can use in various areas. Many of these services are promoted with harm in mind as it could include misleading or false data.

   You can still promote financial services on AdWords, but you would have to list an appropriate disclosure on your site referring to your work. This includes data about how you are marketing your work and what makes it potentially valuable to customers.

Know the limits of whatever it is you are trying to market. You must ensure you are not trying to highlight any content that might be illegal, harmful, or dangerous.

Chapter 32 – Copyright or Trademark Authentication

Are you trying to use copyrighted content to promote your site? For instance, you might be telling people online that you are looking to sell Rug Doctor vacuum cleaners. You would want to say that you have cleaners of this brand and that you want to use the keyword "Rug Doctor vacuum cleaners".

It might take some time to get your content approved due to the copyrighted and trademarked nature of the Rug Doctor name.

You can ask for certification to use a copyright on your AdWords messages. This is a fast-track to have the right to use a brand name or other copyright on Google. The process is vital because some ads might be more effective if you use copyrights or trademarks.

There are several steps you can use to obtain the authentication to use certain copyrights or trademarks:

1. You must first get a license document that states that you have access to copyrighted content.

    For instance, if you are an authorized Rug Doctor vacuum cleaner salesperson, you might have been given full licensing from Rug Doctor to sell their products. You can use that document in this case. You might have to contact the company to obtain that document. Ask the company whose products you are selling to provide you with a license document for selling products. Make sure you get this in writing.

2. Go to the Copyright Documentation Web Form at https://support.google.com/adwords/contact/copyright to start the process.

   The URL includes the appropriate documentation that you can use to obtain authorization.

3. Enter your name, contact email, and AdWords customer ID.

4. Scan a copy of the license document onto your computer and then send it to Google. The document should be signed as approved. The document must state that you have the right to use the content that has been copyrighted for advertising.

5. Enter the name of the company.

6. Add the URLs that contain the copyrighted content that you are wanting to advertise.

7. State if you are the copyright holder.

   If you are not the copyright holder, you should say that you have the permission of the copyright holder to promote and sell the product. You might have to explain in detail what you are doing. Be as specific as possible.

8. Confirm that everything you are providing to Google is accurate and true.

9. Allow Google to contact you in some fashion - by phone or email. The time it takes for you to get a response will vary.

This process is essential to ensure that you avoid any legal issues.

Chapter 33 – Using the Search Network

An interesting part of Google AdWords is that you don't necessarily have to get your ads to show up on the Google search engine alone. You can get extra help when you get your content to other sites that link to Google. This is thanks to what the Search Network offers.

The Search Network that Google uses is a key part of what makes AdWords useful. This is a grouping of websites and apps where your ads can appear. This helps you to make your content more visible outside the standard Google ads you might already use.

The Search Network operates with a simple series of steps:

1. Select to have your ads appear on the Search Network.

2. Your ads will then appear on certain pages that are operated by Google.

   These pages include Google Maps and Google Shopping among others. Any site that has Google in its URL is considered a partner in the Search Network.

3. Any search sites that partner with Google for displaying ads can also be a part of the Search Network.

   This includes many search engines that might be on websites that work outside of Google. These include engines that use the Google mainframe for powering a private search that is focused on one particular website.

What Ads Appear on the Search Network?

The types of ads that you can find on the Search Network include many valuable options for promoting your content:

- Basic text ads

- Dynamic sitelink ads, including the automated extensions you would use

- Call-only ads

- Shopping ads

- Some image or video ads may be supported

If it is something that airs on Google, it will probably work on other sites throughout the Search Network. You have full control over which specific ads that you might want to use.

Have the Search Network Work For You

The best part of using the Search Network is that you only need a few steps to get this part of the Google experience to work for you:

1. Go to the Settings section of your campaign.

2. Select the campaign, ad group or another setup that you will have your ads added onto.

3. Click the Networks option.

4. Select to include your ads in Google search partners.

5. Click on the Save button.

After this, it should be easy to prepare your content when used right. It can be attractive for getting everything laid out properly.

Things to Know

There are a few things that you need to be aware of to use this part of the Google system:

- Although some pictures may be used on some ads on the Search Network, they are completely optional. The Search Network focuses mainly on text ads.

- Your ads might appear on sites within the Search Network that you don't want to use. Keep your keywords as focused on your site content as possible so the odds of this happening will be minimal.

- The Quality Score of your ads ensures that your ads will more likely show up on Search Network partner sites.

When to use the Search Network

It is best to use the Google Search Network when you have a limited budget to work with. When you use the Search Network, you will easily get your content out to more places, but it will not be as wide-spread as the Display Network that you will read about later.

It is also perfect to use this network if you have some kind of product that people need for emergency purposes. Many people might search for services from electricians, plumbers and many others in the emergency services field. People could go find these groups from outside Google. A person might type in details through a local search engine that focuses on a certain community but is powered by Google.

Chapter 34 – Using the Display Network

Have you ever noticed some advertisement online? Maybe you have noticed an ad that is related to the keywords that you might have searched for recently. This ad could appear in a box somewhere on a page. Maybe you might even notice an ad on the side of a YouTube video that you are watching.

These are all examples of ads that come from the AdWords Display Network. This is a distinct part of the AdWords experience that you can use.

Note: To make the Display Network useful to you, you have to create a display campaign. This will be covered in the next chapter.

What Makes the Display Network Different?

Although the names sound familiar, there is a big difference between the Display Network and the Search Network. The Search Network works with many different search engines, and the Display Network focuses on other websites that have enabled support for the AdWords service.

The Display Network is made with a distinguished layout:

1. To start, you would have to create a visual ad - an image or video or another type of ad.

2. The ad will be linked to the keywords that you are using in your ad group.

3. The Display Network will then integrate your ad into a website. This will work based on either place someone has visited recently or the context of the ad is highlighted.

4. The ad will display prominently somewhere on a site.

For most places, it will appear in the form of a visual ad in a box or other spot with a clearly visible layout. For YouTube, the ad will appear as a link to a search or on another listing of videos on the site.

As with other marketing options, you have the choice to get Google AdWords to link your content to other places on the Display Network based on keywords, demographics and much more.

How to Get An Ad Set Up

The process for getting your ad to appear on the Display Network is similar to what you would do to get your content to show on the Search Network:

1. Select the ad group or campaign that you wish to use.

2. Choose the Networks option for how your content will appear.

3. Select that you want your ads to appear on the Display Network.

Remember that this only works for advertisements that can handle the Display Network. These include ads that you will use for a display campaign.

Before Using the Display Network

Although the Display Network itself is convenient and useful for marketing, you have to be careful how your ads will appear on the network. Several things should be planned ahead of time before getting your content to work on the network:

*   The Display Network works best for people who want to introduce themselves to others online.

The Display Network concentrates on content that is easy to spread. You can choose on which sites you want your content to appear.

- The network is suitable when you have an extensive sales process.

  Many advertisements that appear on the Display Network are for more complicated products or services, such as real estate sales, car sales, home renovation services etc.

- You might spend less on an advertisement when you use the Display Network.

  Because the Display Network requires more effort to create a display campaign, you might have less competition. This could result in spending less money on each click.

- With the Display Network, your reach will be larger as more people will notice what you are promoting.

- You can choose to pay for your exposure through either the cost per click or the cost per thousand impressions.

- A display ad on the Display Network is much more visually appealing than something you might use on a site.

- You might have to spend more to get an ad ready on the Display Network because of the cost associated with hiring a designer to help you produce an ad.

How to Exclude Certain Sites

Perhaps there will be certain websites on which you do not want your ads to run. You might feel that these ads are not appropriate for or that you just don't agree with what the site represents. You have the right to exclude certain sites from your AdWords campaign. The exclusion ensures that your content will not be visible to audiences that would not have interest in your content.

1. Go to the ad campaign or group that you wish to use.

2. Go to the Audiences section of the page.

3. Click on the Exclusions tab.

4. Enter the websites that you want to exclude from your ads.

Linking Your Work to YouTube

YouTube is one of the most important members of the Display Network. It is so essential and popular that it is deserving of its own very special section in this chapter.

YouTube is operated by Google and is a prominent place for online videos. You can find any kind of video on YouTube. The search setup also makes it easy for people to find content on YouTube.

You can work with your own YouTube account if you have one to track information on how people are interacting with your content.

1. Sign into your YouTube account.

2. Click on the channel icon or name on the top part of YouTube that you are using. Make sure the channel you wish to link to AdWords is the correct one.

3. Go to the My Channel section and then the Video Manager option.

4. Click the Advanced section under the Channel panel.

5. Click to link the account to AdWords.

6. Go to the Linked Accounts section of AdWords and check on the particular channels that are linked to your AdWords account.

7. At this point, your channel should appear linked to AdWords.

Chapter 35 – Running a Display Campaign

The Display Network that Google offers is convenient and worthwhile, but to make it work for you, it is imperative that you develop your own display campaign.

A display campaign lets you run many ads online in various forms.

When you use a display campaign, you will offer pictures and other images that will link to your site. You can use images that display products you want to sell or things that illustrate services you have to offer. Whatever you use in your display campaign, plan something that has a special and dynamic look to it.

Developing Your Display Campaign

1. Go to the Campaign section of your AdWords account.

2. Click on the Plus sign to indicate you want to set up a new campaign.

3. Select the Display option.

4. List information on the goal of the campaign.

   You can choose to get one of the following as a goal:

   • Drive in sales - This is best when you have basic products to sell.

   • Get leads through email sign-ups or other ways how you can get contacts.

     Use this option if you have some high-value services that you need to market. This includes working with something that might take a while to sell but would require more people to know what you have to offer.

- Bring in website traffic.

- Product or brand exposure - to encourage people to choose your brand and see what it has to offer.

- Brand awareness.

You do not have to work with a goal, but if you have a goal, make sure it relates to the main objective you have. You can add a new goal later to your campaign if you prefer.

5. Choose a subtype for your campaign. You can use either a standard display campaign or a Gmail campaign.

   The standard campaign focuses on having your ads appear on various sites within the Display Network. The Gmail campaign includes ads that can be shown to people as they look through their Gmail accounts. Be advised that you cannot change this section on your campaign after you make a choice.

6. Enter your business website. Google can provide you with ideas for keywords that you can use based on what your site lists. Your keyword ideas will appear when you get your ad groups set up.

7. Enter the name of your campaign.

8. Select the location or locations that you wish to target.

   The process for doing this is the same as a standard search. Be sure to use the right locations and to use the Advanced Search section to get specific ideas on what places you can include or exclude.

As you adjust the locations and other features, the approximate number of impressions you get will increase or decrease. The right-hand side of the screen will give you details on how your targeting reach is changing based on the ads you are producing.

9. Enter the languages you want to use.

   AdWords will give you recommendations based on the places you are targeting. If you want to target both the United States and Canada, you might be encouraged to add French to go with English. Only use the languages that you know you your customers speak.

10. Decide on a bidding campaign - bid on the conversions, clicks, or viewable impressions.

11. List the daily budget. Set the delivery method for standard or accelerated marketing.

12. Enter a name for your first ad group.

13. Include information about the audiences you wish to reach.

    You can target audiences based on how they interact with your content. You can focus your content on people who have interacted with your content. You have full control over what you want to do with your content in this case.

14. List the demographics that you want to reach - gender, age, household income and parental status. Watch how the number of impressions on your campaign changes based on the demographics.

15. Choose the keywords and topics that you want to use.

Part of this includes creating a custom intent audience for your campaign. This will be discussed later.

The key to working with topics is to market your work to people who are interested in specific things. You can select certain targets by choosing the individual topics of value to you. For instance, a video game console retailer can select the Consumer Electronics section, the Computers and Electronics subsection, and then the Game Systems and Consoles option.

Go as deep as you can when choosing these keywords and topics so you can only target people who actively want to search for what you are selling or offering. This reduces the unwanted clicks you might get.

16. Choose the placements for the campaign - can include specific websites, YouTube pages or other spots where you specifically want your ad to appear. Enter the keyword or topic that you want to promote and then you will get recommendations for the placements you can use within your campaign.

17. Select the automation that you will use in the campaign – conservative or aggressive.

You can use a conservative approach when you are trying to stay close to your cost per customer. An aggressive reach gives you more flexibility in your cost while getting more people to react.

18. Add the maximum cost per click or another cost of a parameter that you wish to use.

19. Create a new ad now or just click the Create Campaign button and get the new ad applied later.

Create an Ad Group

You will have to create a new ad group before you can get your campaign running. Fortunately, the process for doing this is easy:

1. Click to create an ad group while on your campaign page.

2. Provide a name for your ad group.

3. Decide on the audiences you want to reach.

4. Review the demographics, content keywords, placements, and other features you will use. You have the option to use the same ones that you used when you created your campaign, but each ad group you use can include its own specific parameters.

5. Decide on the ad group bid you will use.

6. Start creating your new ad.

This leads to the next process.

Creating a Responsive Ad

When you create an ad for this type of campaign, you are specifically going to create a responsive ad. This is a type of message that concentrates on an image that adds a striking look that fits perfectly with your message.

1. Go to the ad group in which that you want to produce an ad.

2. Click on the option to add your responsive ad.

3. Add your own image.

You can upload your own image or scan your website for an image. You can also use a stock image provided by Google provided you enter your URL. Be sure that whatever you plan on using is something that you can legally use.

The image should meet the requirement for a good display. You can use a 1200x1200 or a 1200x628 image or something smaller provided the ratio of the dimensions are the same.

For a logo, you can create a 1200x300 or 1200x1200 image or something smaller with the same ratio.

Google will let you know if it notices any errors on your images as you upload them. Make sure anything you use is carefully laid out and that it has a striking appearance.

4. Enter a short headline of 25 characters.

5. Add a long headline of 90 characters.

6. Use a description of up to 90 characters.

7. Add the name of your business of up to 25 characters.

8. List the final URL for the ad.

9. Enter any tracking templates or custom parameters that you want to use in your ad.

10. You can also add a Call to Action text at the bottom. This can be "Learn More," "Install" or "Visit Site" among other choices.

The best part of creating this type of ad is that it can include a special layout that is unlike anything you could ever see online.

Upload an Ad

The process of creating a responsive ad focuses on what you can do for creating an ad that Google can prepare for you. But what if you want something a little more dynamic? Maybe you have a customized ad that you have already created that you want to showcase. If this is so, you can upload an existing ad that you have already prepared.

When you upload the ad, you can create something that has a more striking and dynamic appearance to it.

1. Go to the ads section of your specific campaign or ad group.

2. Choose the Upload Display Ads option.

3. Click on the Choose Files to Upload section.

4. Select a JPG, GIF, or PNG file that you will use. You can also upload an HTML5 ad through a ZIP file.

    Make sure the ad contains the proper content and has a design that looks professional. You might need to hire someone to professionally produce an ad, but that is your decision.

5. Enter the URL you will use in the ad. Make sure the URL is relevant to the ad you are creating.

Creating a Custom Intent Audience

An exciting feature of a display campaign is creating a custom intent audience. This is a kind of audience that will actively want to search for something you are offering. You can use this at any point in your campaign.

1. Go to the Keywords section.

2. Click to work with the custom intent audience.

3. Enter an audience name that you wish to target.

4. Add the keywords that you wish to target.

5. Look at the Ideas section to the side of the screen to see what keywords might work best.

6. Compare the keywords you select with the audience size on the right side of the screen.

7. Click the Create button after you are finished producing your custom intent audience.

This audience will make your content visible to more people.

Don't forget when using your custom intent audience that you decide whether you want your keywords to appear in an audience or content format.

An audience format means that your ads are to be shown to people who would be likely to be interested in the keywords you are entering. These include people who have searched for things based on those keywords or have online profiles that have expressed interest in what you are marketing. This is a recommended option for your marketing plans.

You can also use content keyword marketing to only show ads on web pages, apps, and videos that are related to the keywords you have chosen.

Working With Extensions

As with a standard AdWords campaign, you can use extensions on your display ads. But the process of getting these extensions is a little different.

You will only be able to use three types of extensions on your AdWords display campaign:

1. Call extensions

2. Location extensions

3. Affiliate location extensions

The good news is that the process for getting these extensions prepared on your display ads will be the same as what you would use for other tasks. Refer back to the chapter on extensions if you need to be reminded of how to get these extensions planned.

The extensions that you produce will be listed next to the main advertisement you are using. This should be useful if you want to get your content to be more attractive and useful.

The big point about working with a display advertisement on AdWords is that it is relatively similar to what you would get out of a basic setup. But the most important point is that you will work with more visual content. Be sure you look at how well you can get your content laid out while making your display campaign look more attractive an intriguing in any fashion.

Tips for a Display Campaign

You can design a quality display campaign any way you want, but the process entails more than just getting some attractive ads set up:

1. Create display ads that come in many sizes.

   Work with more sizes so it becomes easier for your content to be visible on a larger array of pages. You can create ads in sizes from 300x250 to 200x200 to 728x90 among others. Aim to produce at least three size variants of your ads.

2. Keep your campaigns limited.

Think about how you will use only a certain series of keywords on your ads at the beginning. Limit the number of keywords so you can decide which ads might be more appealing.

3. Keep the cost per click on your campaign down if possible.

Use a CPC cost of 30 percent less than your regular search CPC. People are less likely to advertise with display campaigns.

4. Make sure you use the proper exclusions.

Regarding the Display Network, you will need to exclude your ads from sites that you might feel are not appropriate. You can always focus on just targeting very specific sites within a category, but targeting a broad audience is fine at the beginning provided that you specify the right exclusions so your content will be easier to use.

A Few Helpful Tips

There are a few tips that you should use when making a display campaign work:

- Make sure you hold full ownership of anything you want to use. Use your own personal images or videos.

- Keep the quality of your photos or videos as strong as possible. High-definition videos and detailed high-resolution images indicate that you are a professional.

- Always use something that draws someone's attention without looking desperate.

  Someone should want to watch your ad or see what you have to offer. Make sure the language or imagery you use is detailed and unique without sounding overly needy.

- See how your content will look on many devices.

  Check on how your videos and photos will look on both large and small screens. The content must be easy to read and distinguished.

- Work with enough formats over how images will look.

Whether it has a standard box, a rectangle, or even a small sliver, you should find ways to create many advertisements. By doing this, you are creating ads that will be more attractive and appealing.

Chapter 36 – Running a Shopping Campaign

Have you ever taken a look at a listing where you see pictures of products for sale? Maybe you wanted to search for digital media players and you saw a lot of pictures at the top. These pictures might have been for some of the hottest new media players on the market. After the pictures, you can get information on what each product costs, who sells it, and the URL that you can visit.

Marketing on Google is popular because it lets people share information on what they are selling in a dynamic fashion. Best of all, you can get started with your own shopping campaign to make your content visible.

To create a shopping campaign:

1. First, list a series of products that you have for sale through AdWords.

2. Upload images of your products including information on the names, prices and other details.

3. Place a bid on a keyword. This should include a keyword that is relevant to your products that you are selling.

4. People will see your product for sale after finding a keyword relating to it. Your product will compete with other products in the same field. For instance, one pair of hiking boots you have for sale through a shoe store might be displayed by competitors.

5. When someone clicks on your picture or product, that person will be lead to your site.

6. You will be charged for the click that comes onto your site. There is a better chance for you to get a profit from the process if the person who clicks on the link buys the product you have for sale.

The shopping campaign is for physical products. While you might offer services or non-physical products, the shopping campaign is not intended for those points.

The best part of making a shopping campaign is that you will get more qualified leads from your searches. When you get in touch with people, they will notice that you have some quality products and they can see the visual features of whatever you are selling.

CPC-Only

Your shopping campaign is a CPC-only campaign. There are two ways that you will pay when someone lands on your page:

1. First, a user will have to click on an ad that will go a landing page of your website that you specify.

2. Second, the user can click on something that goes to a landing page for your local inventory. This is provided the page is hosted by Google.

The process for bidding on keywords with this kind of campaign is the same as for any other marketing strategy you use. The good news here is that you have full control over deciding what you will spend on each click that is made. You only have to pay the minimum to rate higher than another advertiser who is right behind you.

Where Will the Ads Show Up?

Your ads will appear on a typical search and also on Search Partner sites. The ads will still be at the top of a search.

You can also get your ads to appear on a Google Shopping search (assuming it is in the right country). Google Shopping is a system where people can search for items and then get detailed results on products. Go to shopping.google.com to access Google Shopping.

When you search for things on Google Shopping, you will more than likely come across many paid advertisements. These ads will include all the details that one has on a Google Merchant account including details on the product name, price, the business selling it, and an image of that product.

Which Countries?

Shopping ads on AdWords are not available in all countries. Google offers shopping campaigns and ads in most major countries including the United States, Canada, United Kingdom, Australia, Japan, Brazil, Germany, France, South Africa, New Zealand, and Italy among others.

This service is not available in South Korea, China, Mexico, Kenya, or Egypt. It is not available in most smaller countries like Luxembourg or Ivory Coast.

Requirements for Your Campaign

Before you can start your AdWords campaign, you have to meet all the necessary requirements to get AdWords to work for you. The requirements for your AdWords campaign are as follows:

1. You must have links to AdWords and the Google Merchant Center.

   The Google Merchant Center helps you have your content available on Google. This simplifies the AdWords process by allowing you to upload data of your products and services for sale to Google. The setup lets you send information on prices, features, names, photos, and much more. This allows your content to be easy to find on a Google search.

   Go to merchants.google.com to learn more about how this works. You will also see how to get your Merchant Center account linked to AdWords.

2. Your content must comply with all the shopping policies that Google lists.

   The policies are similar to the rules relating to the content when creating links and advertisements. You would be restricted as to what you can sell based on where you are located and who you are targeting. You must also avoid misrepresenting anything you have on your site or else you may be removed.

3. You must also send regular updates on your product data.

   You will have to send information on your products to Google every 30 days for your listings to remain current. The updates you provide on your product data can include details on what types of products you have for sale and how you will offer them to the public. Be sure to list as much detailed information on your products as possible so Google can continue to have your ads appear online.

The product data specifications are what you will use for getting your content sent to Google. This will be discussed later in this chapter to help you know how to get your content to move out accordingly.

4. If you live in the European Economic Area or Switzerland, you must have a membership with a Shopping Comparison Service or CSS.

   Many CSS options will let you manage your content, but others might have to run your campaigns for you. Check with the CSS you wish to work within the European Economic Area (Switzerland is not an official member of the EEA, but Google includes it for this intention).

Starting Up a Shopping Campaign

After you get online to AdWords, you can start up your own shopping campaign. The rules for doing so are as follows:

1. Go to the menu to create a new campaign.

2. Select the Shopping option.

3. Select the goal that you wish to use. Again, you can change this goal later if desired.

   Choose sales, leads or website traffic.

4. Apply for a Merchant Center account.

   You must have a Google Merchant Center account to take advantage of the AdWords shopping campaign process. The Merchant Center provides you with a platform where you can upload store and product information to Google. The content can be used on AdWords and other services Google offers.

5. Go to merchants.google.com if you do not have a Merchant Center account.

   Be sure to use this service to list information on your website and that you have certain products for sale. You might have to upload information on individual products manually. This includes details on the names, descriptions, prices, etc. Images of the products you are selling might have to be listed here. Refer to the Merchant Center website for instructions on how to do this.

6. After getting your Merchant Center account, click on the Account Linking section.

7. Select the AdWords option and then enter your AdWords ID.

8. Click on the Link option.

9. Go to the Linked Accounts section of AdWords and then use the Google Merchant Center option.

10. Click to approve the pending connection you are using.

    At this point, your Merchant Center account will be fully linked to your campaign. You should have access to details on the products that will be included in your AdWords campaign provided those products have been properly listed within your Merchant Center listing.

11. Enter details on the country where your products are sold.

    You are only able to ship your products to one country within your campaign. If you have products to ship to people in the United States, create one shipping account that targets people in that country. You would need another campaign for people in Canada, another for the United Kingdom and so forth.

12. Use the inventory filter to select the products you will sell.

You can use this option to limit what you will include in a campaign. You might limit the number of products available to keep the cost of running your campaign from being too expensive. You can always adjust your campaign later to focus on products that more people have chosen to respond.

13. Enter the bidding information.

You can prepare a daily budget while also using different bidding totals for each product that you will include in your campaign. Be prepared to change these totals if need be.

14. Set up a campaign priority.

You can add this later if desired, but it helps to have this for when you are advertising a product within many shopping campaigns. Details on how to make this work are covered later in this chapter.

15. Prepare the network that you will use through search partners or through the Google Search Network.

16. Adjust the devices that you will target, the locations you will target and other specifics of your campaign.

You can adjust these things for individual ad groups that you create later. You can still use this to decide where your ads will go and if your content will appear on mobile devices, desktop displays or both.

You will have to look at the type of ad group you will create within this campaign. The next point of this chapter concentrates on how to do this.

Choosing the Right Kind of Ad Group

You have to select a certain ad group that fits with the product you are trying to promote. There are two kinds of ad groups you can use on your shopping campaign on AdWords:

1. Product Shopping Ad

    A product ad is best for newcomers. This is an ad that focuses on an individual product. The ad will be produced automatically based on the content listed on your Merchant Center account. This does well for creating more ads, but you should see that the content you have is clearly labeled and professionally organized.

    To create this ad, go to the ad creation section and choose a product shopping ad. You can use keywords and negative keywords for this ad group just as you would use elsewhere.

2. Showcase Shopping Ad

A showcase ad will have many products in your Merchant Center account all in one ad.

Creating a Showcase Shopping Ad Group

Although a basic shopping ad is easy to use with Merchant Center, a Showcase ad is a little more complicated. With a basic ad, your content will appear alongside the work of other people who are competing with you for the same keyword. However, with a showcase ad, you will have your products appear on their own without any competitors. This is a special choice that provides you with a good way for getting your work to stand out.

A showcase ad: A person will tap on your link via a mobile device. This includes a link that you have connected to a keyword you are bidding on.

When the person accesses the content on your post, that person will see pictures and names of many products you have for sale. Details on the prices and even any customer ratings will be included as well. Whatever you have posted onto your Merchant Center account should appear on this part of your campaign to create a better approach to your ads.

1. Upload a 1:1 logo into your Merchant Center account if you have not done so already.

   This logo will add a better appearance to your ad. It can appear next to the name of your business.

2. Select the shopping campaign in which your ad group will be.

3. Select the showcase ad group option when you create this new ad group.

4. Enter a name for the group and a bid.

   You will pay for your bid when someone clicks on your ad to expand it and views the ad for at least ten seconds or if that person clicks a link on your ad.

5. Establish rules for the product groups that you will highlight.

   Select very specific types of products you want to sell. This includes certain products that link to particular keywords. A shoe store might have one ad group that concentrates on hiking boots, another for ladies' sandals and another for boys' sneakers. You will also have to exclude certain product groups that you do not want to include in your content.

6. Click on the Save button to Save the ad group.

At this point, you will create a new ad that fits in with the ad group you wish to use.

Creating a Showcase Ad Within Your Ad Group

At this stage, you will have to set up a new ad that will fit in with your ad group. This showcase ad can be created immediately after you get the initial ad group ready, but you can create a new ad separately later if you wish.

1. Add a header image for your ad.

   The header image should be the one that will represent whatever it is you are including in that group. Be sure the image is large and detailed enough while having at least one of the products you want to sell listed in that ad. Avoid anything with watermarks, identifying bits of texts, or anything else that might make the advertisement unattractive.

   A good idea for your header image is to use something that reflects the many products that you have to offer - something symbolic of what makes your products or services beneficial.

2. Review the product images that you wish to use.

The product images should be the ones that are already in your Merchant Center account. You can add new ones if you prefer.

3. Add a headline and a description to the ad.

4. List the final URL to which the link will go.

5. Enter the display URL that you will show.

   It does not have to be the exact same as the final URL. It just needs to be something that is attractive to readers and shows what you have to offer in some fashion.

6. Take a look at your ad by previewing it on the right-hand side of the screen.

7. Click to Save the ad after you are finished making changes.

Note: You will have to wait to get your content to load on AdWords. Google has to review your advertisement to see that the content is legitimate and that your website is running as well as it should. You might have to wait about two to three business days to get confirmation, but the timing will vary.

Managing Your Product Data Specification

To keep your ads running on AdWords, you must regularly provide the product data specification on your products through the Merchant Center. By doing this, you are submitting information on your products to Google for review. Google needs regular updates to keep your data consistent and active. More importantly, Google needs this to ensure that you are direct with your products and that the listings you are working with are accurate and appropriate.

Note: The data specifications you are using will be vital to keeping your content on AdWords. You must still keep all other parts of your online retail page active and updated for Google to accept it. These include parts relating to your landing page, your shipping plans, any tax rates you use, shipping rates, and language or currency applicable to your site.

How to Submit Your Data

You must use these steps to submit your content:

1. Log into your Merchant Center account.

2. Check the data that links to your products for sale. Make sure the content is filled out and that all required forms have been completed.

3. Use the submission section of your Merchant Center to move your content to Google.

4. Google will then review and confirm the data.

5. At this point, you can get the content to link to your AdWords account.

This should make your work accessible and functional. But to make it work, you must plan out all the data that you will use in your account to make it operational. This gives you more control over how your content will be laid out and utilized.

Key Data to Submit

You must work with the appropriate amounts of data for planning your content. The data that you must use in this situation entails the following points so you can get your ad listed properly:

1. ID - An identifier should be used for each product you will promote on AdWords. It is best to use the SKU number for the product if possible. You might be selling a shoe from a particular company that has an SKU listed on it. List that identifying stock keeping unit number. You can also use the UPC if applicable. This can be up to 50 characters long, so it should be easy to prepare for any product you are selling.

2. Title - The title includes a description of a product. If you are offering a boot for men in a shoe store, ad information could be "Men's Brown Leather Boot." This can be up to 150 characters long. Make sure the content is accurate and that it includes details on distinguishing features of whatever you are selling. Don't use gimmicky words in your title.

3. Description - The description can be up to 5,000 characters long and includes more details of a product for sale. For the men's brown leather boot, you could list information on what that boot is made of, the type of sole, any aeration features, how you can clean it and so forth. Adding enough detail is important, but it should still be accurate. This should not include any links to your store or details on any sales. The description must only focus on the product you are trying to sell to without being pushy or promotional in the process.

4. Link - The link is the landing page for the product you are selling. This is not the front page or some page of a generic section, but rather a page that concentrates solely on what you are selling. This works best when an encoded URL is used.

5. Image Link - The image of your product must also be included with a URL link to that image. The image must accurately show whatever you are selling without including promotional text or unwanted content.

6. The availability of your product - State that your product is either in stock, out of stock, or is being preordered. Keep a careful eye on your inventory.

7. Price - Always enter the regular price of your product. You do not have to list the sale price.

8. Product Category - For example, men's boots, you can use a category listed on the Merchant Center that refers to apparel followed by clothing and then something for shoes. Go as far deep into this as possible.

9. Brand Identifier - You must enter information on the brand of your product. If you are selling boots from Columbia, enter that brand. This can be up to 70 characters long.

10. GTIN - The Global Trade Item Number must be included. This should be the UPC for your product. It would be the EAN in Europe or the JAN in Japan. For a book, the ISBN would be used.

11. Condition - List this as being new, used, or refurbished.

12. Adult Status - You would use this if the product you are selling is designed with suggestive use for adults. Google will adjust your AdWords experience to ensure that the product is only promoted to people who are of legal age.

Various other additional parameters may be included based on the product you are selling. This includes information on the size, the year that a product was made, etc. The Merchant Center will guide you through the process.

Regardless of what you are selling, you should always keep your content active. This is to let AdWords see that you have legitimate products for sale and that there is enough information for people to see what you are offering.

Optional Items

The points in this listing are not things that you absolutely have to include in your listing for AdWords and in the content you are submitting to AdWords. These can still help make your ads more descriptive and appropriate.

1. Additional Image Link

   This is an optional feature that lets you add a link for a second image relating to your product if you want to promote your work with up to ten pictures. This is perfect if the product you are selling is very detailed and needs extra information posted online.

2. A Mobile Landing Page - where someone would go when clicking on a product using a mobile device.

3. Date When an Item Is Available - when you are using the "preorder" setting for availability.

4. Sale Price - This is optional if the price might only be at that rate for a limited time. You can also add information on the effective dates for the sale price.

There are far too many other options to add to your content. The choices will vary based on the product you are offering.

A Campaign Priority

Campaign priority is a part of shopping ads that may help to get certain ads to be highlighted above others. You might have multiple campaigns where you are trying to sell the same kind of product to people in the same country. With campaign priority, you will list details on the ad that you want to have appear in your listing above all else.

This works best with shopping campaigns, but it may also work well for other types of campaigns. You can have a low priority set to a search campaign and a high priority for a display one, for instance. This can be useful when trying to make your content stand out and be more useful.

To get the campaign priority organized:

1. First, the campaign that you list as having a higher priority will be the one that bids on keywords first. This ruling works even when the campaign with the higher bid value is one with a lower priority.

2. When the budget for the high-priority campaign runs out, the ads for the next one on the priority list will start running.

3. The highest bid will be used if you have many campaigns that are of the same priority.

How to Adjust the Priority

Several steps should be used to control the priority of your ads for a shopping campaign:

1. Go to the campaign page for the one that you will adjust the priority.

2. Go to the Settings menu.

3. Choose the campaign priority option.

4. Select the priority that you want to use. You can go for a high, medium, or low priority.

5. Click on the Save icon.

6. Use this process with all the other campaigns whose priorities you wish to adjust.

Ideal for Sales

Don't forget to think about the sales or other special offers you have when setting the priority plans. You should give anything that you have on sale higher priority. You can also use this for promoting items that might be more popular based on how many people visit certain parts of your site or how many times something has been purchased.

You will have to adjust the priority levels on your own to make this work.

Local Inventory Ads

Are you looking to promote a product that you currently have available for sale at a physical location? You can use a local inventory ad to target people in a local area based on what is available on certain websites. This is an ad that you will direct to a mobile device.

Your shopping ad will include a simple design:

1. A person will find your product on a mobile search.

2. After tapping on your listing, the ad will include details on a local retailer that is offering the product for sale.

3. The phone then has links to call the store that offers something, get directions to a certain place, or to buy a product online.

This is perfect to promote products in your store and to make your store get its own online presence. You can also use this to review how your ads will lead to in-store sales at a physical spot that you are promoting.

How to Get Local Inventory Ads Ready

There are a few steps you must use to produce your local inventory ads so they will stand out and read well:

1. Get all the necessary accounts for using Google AdWords and the Merchant Center ready. Have your content linked up to Google Maps.

2. Enable your local inventory ads. Go to your Merchant Center account and click on the Get Started option on the local inventory ads part of the programs section.

3. Click on the Enable button to start the local inventory ads provided you have met all the qualifications for getting your site loaded correctly.

4. Create a feed highlighting your local products.

   The points you would have to include in this section will vary based on the type of product you have.

5. Register your local feeds for products you have at your site. This includes details on any inventory reports you have.

   The products on your local inventory reports should accurately match the types of products that you want to market on your site.

6. Have your inventory verified.

   You will have to enter your local inventory ads onto the Merchant Center and then click on the program bar to request verification. Google will review your feeds and the products you have and information on any particular locations you are going to use.

7. Once the content has been verified, you can go to the shopping settings in your Merchant Center account to link your content to AdWords.

This process takes extra time, but it helps get your AdWords account to use the local inventory data that you are using. Be sure to check on how your AdWords account data loads. This gives you more control over how your work is to be highlighted and made available to the online public.

Chapter 37 – Creating a Video Campaign

Have you ever seen advertisements on YouTube? You probably have seen something showcasing a product or service. A video ad might be more memorable because it provides people with an interesting layout that offers more information.

A video campaign will work with not only YouTube but also other sites within the Display Network that can handle video ads.

People might recall more information from a video campaign than the text on an advertisement.

More importantly, a video campaign lets you get more information out to people. You could use a video campaign to highlight demonstrations of products or services you have for sale. You can also answer questions that people might send by email or on social media.

Types of Video Ads

The interesting thing about marketing your work with YouTube and other video sites is that there are many kinds of videos that you can use. These are ads that all might have different messages and content.

1. **TrueView Ads**

   TrueView ads are the most prominently featured ads on a video campaign. These are ads that will appear before or after or even during a video being played on YouTube or somewhere else on the Display Network. It is very easy to get one of these ads to be noticed because these videos are posted immediately online. Your viewer can skip past the video after five seconds. This makes it critical for you to try and make your video more attractive so that someone will want to keep on watching it after the video starts up.

2. Outstream Ads

An outstream ad will appear on a mobile or tablet device. This would work on a Google partner site. The view can simply tap on the video to have it play.

3. Bumper Ads

A bumper ad is very short in length – six seconds or less - and can be found in the same spots as a TrueView ad. This provides you with a short window to contact someone, but it is also an ad that lets you get people to see your content quicker.

4. TrueView Discovery Videos

A TrueView discovery video only works on YouTube, and someone would have to actively click on the link. After the user clicks on the thumbnail for your ad, that video will start to play on a new screen. Think of this as a voluntary approach, but it is also one where you can get in touch with someone by simply sharing details on what is being offered at any given moment.

Creating Your Video Campaign

You will need to produce good video ads that are dynamic and attractive. They also have to look professional. This includes using high-definition content. Having the video professionally recorded and edited is something to consider.

Once your videos are ready:

1. Select a new campaign option - choose the video section.

2. Specify the goal that you want to attain. You can also choose to have no goals at the time, but you can change that later. You can choose to get leads, website traffic, consideration for your brand or just added brand reach.

3. Select a subtype for your goal. For instance, when you are trying to get leads, you can choose drive conversions.

4. Enter a name for your campaign.

5. Set a budget for what you will spend each day or what you will spend during the life of your campaign.

6. Enter the start and end dates for your campaign.

   You can choose to get your campaign to start as soon as possible. You can also leave the end date blank when you want to highlight something for as long as possible.

7. Select the networks that you want to use.

   You can choose to get your videos to appear on YouTube and on Display Network sites. You also have the option to get your ads to appear next to your search results on YouTube. This is for your discovery ads and requires you to produce proper thumbnails, descriptions, and titles for your videos to make them more useful.

8. Enter the language and location data. Don't forget about the advanced settings like with other campaign options.

9. Select the bidding setup you want.

   Depending on your goal, you will have the option to work with the cost per view, impression, or conversion. Include a total of how much you want to spend on your bids.

10. Use the standard content filter at this point to determine the types of content you don't want your ads to show. This includes working with ratings for your content to appear on videos rated for certain audiences.

    Remember that YouTube uses a platform where some videos can be off-limits to minors or those who do not have accounts on YouTube. You will have to think about who you want to watch your ads.

11. Set up the specific devices on which you want to have your videos display. This includes both desktop and mobile devices.

    This can be changed to the settings section of your campaign later. AdWords puts these options out in front when you start your campaign to make it easier for you to use the options you want to work with.

12. Enter details on how many times your ads can appear within a certain time frame including the number of impressions and views.

13. Add details on when you want to have the ads in your pending ad groups appear. Details on the days of the

week and specific hours for airing your content should be included.

At this point, your campaign should be fully created. You can use the settings section on your dashboard to change some of the parameters that are listed here. This includes choosing to get those settings changed for individual ad groups that you want to produce.

Planning Your Video Ad Groups

Now you need to get video ads to work with your campaign. These video ads should be planned, but you have to get an appropriate ad group ready.

1. Start by creating an ad group. List a name for the ad group and details of the demographics and audiences you want to target based on age, parental status, interests, life events or how they might have interacted with your business in the past.

   Remember that you will target a smaller audience when you are more specific.

2. Enter the keywords that you will use within your video ad group. Add a related website to your keywords to get ideas for what you can target within your campaign.

3. List details on the topics that will be the focus of your ads. Be as specific as possible while using as many smaller sections to concentration on a particular thing.

4. Add placements on certain YouTube channels, websites, or apps.

You also have the option to add many placements by clicking on the proper option to add the placement URLs that you will use. This would work with the Display Network in mind, but you will at least specify that you will want to work with certain kinds of content.

Loading Your Videos

After you get your video ad group ready, you can prepare an actual ad for your content.

1. Start by making sure your AdWords account is linked to your YouTube account.

   Refer to the earlier section in this guide for details on how to get your AdWords account ready for use.

2. Go to the Ads and Extensions section of your video campaign page.

3. Click to create a new ad.

4. Select the ad group that the ad will appear on.

5. Enter the URL for your YouTube video.

   You will have to upload your YouTube video onto your account if you have not done so already.

6. Select the video ad format - in-stream, discovery, bumper, or outstream ad format.

7. Enter the final URL. This is the place that people will go to when clicking on your video.

8. Enter the display URL for the video.

9. Add a ten-character Call to Action on your ad.

10. Include a 15-character headline.

This will appear on a small bar that lists information on who is providing the ad. The Call to Action button will be distinct and provide the user with information on what makes the act distinct.

11. Enter the name of your ad - up to 255 characters long. It should appear around the top part of your ad.

After this, you should have the video ad prepared. This will appear when it is linked to the keywords or other content listed on the ad group to which the video was assigned. Be certain that you've made a good ad that someone is going to recall and will want to share with others.

Planning an Audience for Video Ads

You can target people based on various interesting events that they might have experienced recently.

1. Go to the Audiences section within your ad group or campaign for your video ads.

2. Select the interests or habits of your target audience.

   These interests include things that people hold an affinity for. For example, a travel agent could choose a section focusing on travel and then select the Travel Buffs option to target people who enjoy recreational traveling.

3. Add a customized affinity audience if desired. Click on the Plus button in the affinity section and then add keywords that highlight certain places, apps, URLs, or interests.

The best thing to do here is to add at least five of these points. This narrows down your audience and lets you find people based on specifics.

4. Go to the section on things that people are researching or planning.

5. Select audiences based on life events that they are planning.

   This section highlights certain activities that people might be getting ready to do. For example, select a section for moving so you can target people who are moving soon or have recently moved or target people who plan on getting married or are newly married. The options you have will vary based on your content.

6. List information on how people have interacted with your ads.

   You can include particular keywords you want to focus on in this case. This adds a dynamic approach to handling your content and lets you reach people who might have seen your ads or site recently.

7. After saving your audience information, go to the exclusions tab to select the specific audience members you want to exclude from your content.

You can use as many audiences as you want, but these would be associated with different ad groups and campaigns.

When Will You Be Billed?

You will be billed for your video ads based on many factors:

1. You could be billed when someone clicks on a discovery ad and starts watching it. They will have voluntarily clicked on your ad.

2. For an in-stream video ad, you will pay when someone watches your ad for 30 seconds or the entire duration of the video if it is shorter than that.

   You would have to clearly make your video more appealing so someone will pay attention to the video instead of just skipping over it.

3. Depending on the bidding structure you use, you might pay for a certain number of impressions.

   This is regardless of how long people see your ad or if they notice a thumbnail and description without actually clicking on your content.

What About Extensions?

You only have two extension options for your YouTube ads - either location or affiliate location extensions. You do not have to use either of these extensions in your campaign, but it does help to at least think about how you are going to make that content stand out.

Important Tips for Your Videos

Your AdWords videos can be more successful if you use a few tips. You already know about creating videos that look professional, but you should do a few other things:

1. Get a person's attention as soon as possible within the video.

   Because you don't want someone to skip over your video, you need to find a way to make your video distinct. Provide the most important or valuable information within the first five seconds of your video.

2. For a discovery video, make sure the description and thumbnail look appealing.

   The thumbnail you load up could be a segment of your video, but it might be better to create your own thumbnail and update it yourself through AdWords and YouTube. With a good thumbnail, someone will see what your video is about before clicking on it to watch that production. Also, you can use any kind of description that you want for your video so long as it offers enough information and why the video in question is intriguing.

3. Always make sure the content you are using is original.

   You need to keep your content original and distinct. Do not use other peoples' content. Instead, create your own work.

4. Use as many variants of your ads as possible. Don't repeat the content.

   Have you ever gone online and kept on seeing the same video ad many times? Maybe you got tired of seeing it all the time. Change your ads while using a distinct layout for each one. Create a unique script for each ad while highlighting different things about what you are offering. Adding a variety of ads takes a bit of time, but it makes it easier for people to stay intrigued by your ads.

Your video ads will take some time for you to make, but it is definitely worthwhile if you've got content to highlight that deserves its own video.

Chapter 38 – Universal App Campaign

Everyone loves using mobile applications. They love how they are easy to load onto their mobile devices and how they can be simple to buy and use. In fact, businesses are willing to get their own apps created to make it easier for people to buy things or to learn more about what they have to offer. It is no wonder why so many groups that produce apps are so profitable these days.

You can use a Universal App campaign if you have an app that you want to promote. You can use this with either Android or iOS apps. This is great for when you have a program that you people to download or to make in-store purchases. This could prove to be valuable if you plan your bids properly. Your bids could be worth much less than the cost for someone to spend to get an app installed.

The campaign you use will get your ads to appear on many sites. This can work with ads on the Google Display Network and on YouTube as well as the stores that have your app available. This also does well with regular Google searches. The overall design of the campaign is to create a layout where you can get certain items promoted for downloading.

Note: You will have to create separate campaigns for Android and iOS apps even if you have the same app available on the two separate operating systems. You can always use the same audiences and parameters for each of these campaigns, but you would still have to create separate campaigns.

Starting Your Campaign

You must have an app on the Google Play or App Store depending on the platform you are using.

1. Select the Universal App option.

2. Select the platform for your app - Android or iOS app.

   Remember, AdWords does not support Blackberry, Windows Phone or other small-level operating systems.

3. Enter the name of your app. Click on the specific icon and layout of whatever app you are planning on marketing.

4. Add a name for your campaign.

5. Add up to four text ideas of 25 characters each.

   These lines of text should be separate from one another. Google can use these lines to create ads with different layouts. This creates fresh and unique ads. The best thing to do here is to check the description you have posted on your app to see what you can use.

6. Check the official name of the app and the icon.

   These are two features that you should have created after getting your app loaded onto the App Store or Google Play.

7. Choose to add a YouTube ad if you wish. Enter the URL for the YouTube ad you wish to use, but make sure your account is linked to YouTube for this part of the campaign to work.

8. Load up to twenty images for your ad. This is also optional but makes your content more attractive.

9. Select the locations and languages that you will use.

10. Select the campaign optimization standard that you will use.

The campaign optimization should focus on how well your ad will reach people. You can use this to target all users or users who might be likely to make in-app purchases.

Focus on either the install volume or the in-app purchases that you want people to make when using your app.

11. Add details on the average budget that you will spend each day.

Remember you will pay up to your daily budget times 30.4, the average number of days in a month.

12. Choose to spend your budget either with a standard delivery method or an accelerated layout.

13. Enter the cost per install of your app.

Make sure the total is a reasonable amount that you are willing to spend for each install of your app. Keep the targeted total below the actual value of the app or what would be the profit for an installation.

14. Add the location types that you will target.

15. Select when you are going to run your campaign for. Make it open-ended or with a specific end date in sight.

This is one of the easiest types of campaigns to manage because there are not too many options for use. If anything, the content you will use the most should come from the link that you have on the Google Play or App Store listing that you created. Your app will include all the details, various pictures, and reviews. The ad that you have created will just introduce the readers to your content.

Again, make sure you create a new campaign for the other operating system so that you have the same app included in two separate operating systems. The Android and iOS platforms work with different standards to make them operational and active.

Review the Previews

The previews include reviews of how your ad will look on one of many platforms. This can include a look at your ad through a basic search, a YouTube listing, or on the Display Network.

Which Format Is Best?

There is no real answer as to which format is going to be best for you to use. Although the Android operating system is controlled by Google, you can still use the iOS platform if desired.

Remember that the Android platform has four different spaces where your ads can appear:

1. Google searches

2. On the Google Play store

3. On the Google Display Network

4. YouTube searches

The iOS platform does not work with the Google Play store, obviously. The iOS ad setup does not work with the App Store. However, iOS users will still get access to your ads through AdWords.

With Universal App ads, it becomes easier for your app to be noticed by more people. Be sure to use this for your apps, but make sure you get a campaign prepared for each of the two major operating systems for your app.

Chapter 39 – The Express Platform

The last of the campaigns that you can create through the AdWords platform is the Express option. The Express platform is used when you need to meet certain business goals. This will use automated ads that appear on Google and various other places that Google partners with.

This is an appealing setup that is designed to help you get an ad produced quickly. This does well after you have arranged for your account funding. This is designed as a promotional solution for making a listing very easy to prepare. It might not reach as many people as another type of platform, but this can still be useful for when you are aiming to market your content to people who might be very interested in your work.

Express Platform Set Up

The steps for getting the Express platform to work for you are simple:

1. Select the Express option on the new campaign menu.

2. Choose the action that you want your customers to take.

   You will be given the option to either get people to call your business, visit your physical location, or to take actions on your site. The option you choose will influence the advertisement that comes from your site.

3. Enter the name of your business - up to 120 characters long.

4. List the name of your business website. Only use an appropriate option that fits.

5. Enter details on where you want to target.

   You can target people by certain regions or by a particular radius. You can enter a location and then a targeting radius within a certain number of miles. Notice the stat box on the side that lists details on the potential audience size that you can reach each month.

6. Enter the category of the products or services offered by your business offers.

   You can only choose one option, so choose the one that you know fits in with what you plan on marketing.

7. Add two headlines - 30 characters in length each.

8. Include a description - 80 characters in length.

9. List information on where your ad will go.

   You can use a link to the site that you added earlier in the process of creating your ad, but you can also add a new URL provided that the URL works and that it is related to your ad content and your business.

10. Select your budget.

    You can adjust the indicator on the screen to see what you can spend on average each day plus what the maximum amount you would spend each month. You can compare this with the number of clicks and how many impressions you will get per month. Google will automatically charge you for the clicks based on the average amount of money that people have spent on their ads through this service.

11. Review the content and then click to go forward with the campaign when you are finished.

The ad is now ready for you to use.

The Express Interface

After creating an Express ad, you will be led to a special interface that features a unique layout for how your content will be shown. This includes a layout showing the places you are targeting, the ad you are creating for display, how many people have accessed your content and so forth. You can adjust your content in any way you see fit. You can adjust the search phrases you are working with, how the ad looks and so forth. Experiment with this interface.

Who Should Use the Express Setup?

The Express setup is appealing for those who want to get started with AdWords. At the same time, it does not have as many control features as a basic AdWords campaign or ad group.

You can use this to get your content out to Google quickly. The training that you can get by using the Express layout is always worth using.

Think about how this option for a campaign works when getting your promotional plans ready. Using the Express setup offers a nice way for you to market your content and make it valuable.

Chapter 40 – Working With Salesforce

Salesforce is a popular computing platform that you can use to get information on how well your business is running. With Salesforce, you can get information on the offline conversions that you are getting. This is a necessity to use if you have a physical shop that you are trying to promote online with AdWords. Salesforce does exceptionally well to help you keep tabs on your Analytics even if you have a physical store that is not easy for AdWords to track on its own.

Salesforce will tell you how well you are getting your leads to a transition to actual customers. Salesforce uses its Sales Cloud system to identify how certain keywords and campaigns you are using on AdWords can help you get leads into your store. Best of all, you can link AdWords and Salesforce together to identify how well your store is capable of taking in the leads and content that you are using. By using the right content, you will have an easier time identifying what bits of content are working the best, thus helping you to get a campaign running right without problems.

Planning Salesforce Work

You must get ready for using Salesforce by using a few points for making this program work for you:

1. Obtain the proper permission to use a Salesforce account linked to your site.

2. Use the auto-tagging feature in AdWords. You would have to go into the settings menu of your campaign to turn on this feature.

3. Obtain access to the code for your site. You will need to use this code to get the special GCLID added to your site for tracking purposes.

4. Make sure the process of having a click become a conversion takes less than 90 days.

Any business that has long-term transactions will have to work with a longer conversion plan. Salesforce is not going to work well with anything that takes some time to work.

How to Get Salesforce to Work For AdWords

To have the two systems work together:

1. Get proper accounts with Salesforce and AdWords.

2. Go to the Linked Accounts section of your AdWords account and choose the Salesforce option.

   You will have to get a pop-up window to open to link to your Salesforce page. Be sure your computer allows you to view the ad as it opens up.

3. Log onto your Salesforce account from that window.

4. Follow the prompts in that window after logging in to get the linking function complete.

   The process will authenticate your Salesforce account and ensure the content moves forward to have it synced correctly.

5. As you configure your Salesforce account, you must produce a new GCLID field in your lead objects and other spots you want your AdWords account to link to. This should be used as an Opportunity object.

   The GCLID is the Google Click ID. This ID states that someone came onto your site from an AdWords ad. You can create a field with up to 255 characters to help you distinguish the specific link that you are producing on this site.

6. Adjust the Stage field to allow for field history tracking.

7. Get your Lead object updated with the proper GCLID. Again, activate the field history tracking feature.

8. Insert the GCLID code you want to work with into the code for every page on your site.

   This might take some time, but Salesforce and AdWords will provide you with the full code that you can use. This can be cut and paste all throughout your site to make this work quickly.

9. Create a basic web-to-lead form. Add the fields that you want to add to your program.

   The Salesforce program will help you identify the things that you will use based on the lead you are using. Following the instructions that Salesforce provides.

10. Test your system.

    Add the listing "?gclid="test"" next to your URL. Go to your lead form and send a test lead. After that, check if the test lead is being read on your Salesforce account. Convert that test into an opportunity at this point.

11. After this is fully tested and you have your AdWords and Salesforce accounts linked, set up the conversions that you wish to use.

    Go to the Measurement menu in the settings and then the Conversions section of your campaign. Click on the Salesforce option. Review the new conversion actions that you will use with Salesforce.

You can use many conversion actions including options for new opportunities or lead sales that you wish to read and use. For the best results, keep the maximum conversion window at 90.

12. As everything is prepared, you can get your conversions imported as you see fit.

The Salesforce software program will let you get those conversions organized.

This process is clearly complicated and can be difficult. The best thing to do is to review the Salesforce instructions that are given with your account. Check the Salesforce site to see that it is functional for tracking and if it can work for you.

Chapter 41 – Creating Automated Rules

AdWords can adjust the settings on your account automatically. Automated rules can be programmed in AdWords so that you don't have to make lots of manual changes all the time.

You can use automated rules for producing rules where the prices of bids and other things will change based on certain parameters. By using this, you will make it easier for your account to be adjusted and managed.

The best part is that there is an extensive variety of great rules that you can use:

- You can choose to get a keyword to stop being used if it is not working well on your campaign.

- You can schedule specific ads to appear at certain times based on sales and other special events happening.

- Keyword bids can be raised based on your ranking or lowered if you are high enough or your Quality Score is great.

- You can also get an email or other notification sent to you in the event you are reaching the limit of your daily budget.

You can get up to a hundred of these rules added to your AdWords account and on as many campaigns or groups as you wish.

Creating Rules

First, let's look at the rules involved in getting automated functions to work:

1. While in the middle of a keyword, ad group or campaign section, click on the Automate option.

2. Select a certain rule you wish to use.

AdWords provides many options for this, so look carefully to see what is available.

3. Enter the criteria relating to the rule you want to use.

Be as specific as possible when entering the rule. Also, you must use a percentage number for some of the changes you are making. This can be positive for when you are increasing something and negative for the opposite.

4. Enter how often that automated rule will apply.

You can use the rule for a few hours or even a few days. But the rule will only be active when the parameters you have set are met.

5. Preview the results of your rule before you confirm it.

6. Click the Save button to set the rule.

7. Review the Manage Rules section in the Automate menu to see how the rules are working. Be sure they are working to your liking.

Vital Tips

There are a few sensible tips to use when getting your AdWords automated rules ready:

- Create proper limits on each of the rules that you set up.

Watch for how limits are used so you do not go too high or low in terms of values and other parameters. If you only set a low or high, the other end will remain undefined. This could create something overly complicated or expensive.

- Always preview what your rules feature.

  AdWords will help you review the specific details surrounding any new rules you want to use.

- Check on all the rules that you use within the same group, keyword, or campaign.

  Check on each rule to see that you are not using content that might clash. That is, the content should blend with what you are highlighting.

- See that the content you are working with is sensible based on the type of product or service you are promoting.

  For instance, you might offer banking or financial services, but you might be closed on weekends. You can create rules stating that your ads will not play on weekends. This keeps the ads from being listed in certain situations.

A Quick Note

Although the automated rules that you can generate through AdWords will be useful, you must be cautious. You should always check on your account regularly to see how these rules are working. You should never assume that these rules are going to go through every time. Also, you should adjust your automated rules on occasion. Making the right adjustments can help you get more out of a campaign.

Chapter 42 – Content Exclusions

It is true that your ads can appear on any site that you want as long as they are on the Google Search Network or Display Network or just on Google itself. Sometimes there might be places that you don't want to share your content.

Content exclusions can be used in your AdWords campaign to keep your content from being exposed to places that it might not be suitable. This is important if you want to target people at the right times.

You don't want to be seen as being insensitive. For example, do you think a store that sells party supplies should have an advertisement next to a news website article about war, violence, and death? Also, it would be a bad idea for an ad promoting violent movies or video games to be next to some site highlighting family-related activities that allow parents and kids to have fun together.

Content exclusions ensure that your content is made available at the right times to the best people possible. Google will identify the subject matter and content on a site to determine the audience that is appropriate. It may also identify sensitive content that might require certain warnings.

How to Prepare Your Exclusions

To prepare content exclusions:

1. Select the campaign on which you want to add your exclusions.

2. Go to the Settings menu.

3. Click on the Content Exclusions option.

4. Select the digital content labels on which you want your ads to appear.

This refers to the type of audience that is suitable to view your ad.

5. Select the individual pieces of sensitive content that you want to keep your content from appearing. This may entail a standard content filter if you have a video ad.

6. Enter the types of content for which you do not want your content to appear.

You can choose to keep your content from appearing on games, live-streaming YouTube videos, as part of in-video programs, below the fold on a website and so forth.

7. Click Save to confirm that you do not want your content to appear on all these sensitive places.

Note: AdWords used to allow people to avoid having their ads appear on forums, photo-sharing pages, video-sharing sites, or social media networks. However, as of early 2018, those options are no longer available. Google is working to keep its AdWords content from appearing on those sites altogether. This includes keeping its video-sharing ads to only appear on YouTube because Google owns that service.

Digital Content Labels

Digital content labels will keep your ads from appearing on sites where they might not be appropriate. Think of a content label as if it were one of those ratings you would see on a movie, television program, or video game.

There are six options for digital content labels:

1. DL-G - This is suitable for general audiences. Anyone can see your content.

2. Suitable For Families - This is related to DL-G, but the difference is that the content is specifically with families in mind. It is safe for adults and kids alike.

3. DL-PG - This is good for most audiences, although parental guidance is suggested.

4. DL-T - This for teens and older audiences. It does not have anything adult or mature in nature, but it is not necessarily for younger children.

5. DL-MA - This option is for mature audiences only. It is for things like adult-oriented products or services for the most part.

6. Content Not Rated - This allows you to reach many people, but it could also accidentally get into the hands of someone who is too young or immature to handle your content.

Be cautious when using these ratings. You should only allow your ads to appear on sites that are rated by Google as being appropriate for certain audiences that would be more likely to want to use your product. You should not include an ad for feminine hygiene products on a site that is suitable for families or has a DL-G rating, for instance.

Sensitive Content vs. Standard Content Filters

The standard content filter is used for video campaigns. The sensitive content filter is for things on the Display Network.

While these two are different, they both have the same overall intention in mind. They ensure that your content is not going to appear on sites where your content might be deemed inappropriate for whatever reason.

Although you can choose to block your content from appearing on sites with certain content, remember that these two filters work differently from one another. They have their own definitions for what they will block from a site.

As you review these points, remember:

- The sensitive content filter is for the Display Network.

- The standard content filter is for your video campaign.

1. **Tragedy and Conflict**

   A standard content filter blocks out graphic footage of war, combat and other violent actions. The sensitive filter goes further and blocks out footage relating to war and combat. This includes footage of soldiers marching, people with weapons or shooting those weapons.

2. **Sensitive Social Issues**

   The standard content filter blocks videos that are about controversial topics in society. The sensitive filter eliminates news, videos, and even commentary relating to such topics.

3. **Profanity**

   While the standard filter excludes anything that includes a consistent use of profanity, the sensitive filter will eliminate that content even when it entails things being censored.

4. **Sexually Suggestive Content**

The content includes videos or other data on sex or sex-related items. This includes information on any sex products. The standard filter focuses on basic content, but the sensitive filter stops music videos that contain sexual themes.

5. **Sensational Content**

Sensational content refers to content that includes accidents, disasters, and other events that relate harm. The standard filter excludes videos and content relating to such events that show death and casualties in many forms. The sensitive filter excludes those videos and content plus content that show even the smallest bits of harm or injury.

These restrictions are designed to keep people from having access to content that they might not be comfortable viewing. It is understandable as to why people might be offended by certain content. They might feel as though they are difficult to process or to mentally or emotionally handle. Some might also feel that the content being posted is inappropriate for a household with children.

Consider content exclusions out of respect for your clients, not to mention to keep your content from being in sites where it would clearly not be appropriate. You have an ethical and moral obligation to ensure that your work is not going to be viewed on the wrong spots when trying to make it available on AdWords.

Consider Importance

There is one thing that should be mentioned here. Although it is important to have content exclusions, you need to look at how restrictive you are making your content. You will surely reduce your total audience reach when you have more of these exclusions added to your site.

There are several things you can do to control the exclusions that you are adding:

1. Think about the target audience that would be interested in your content.

   You should only use restrictions on groups that are outside of your target audience. For instance, a website that offers legal information would not do well on a DL-G-rated page or one that is suitable for families. The ad would work best on sites that are rated for people who are a little older and understand the importance of the services being offered by a legal team.

2. Think about the sensitivities of the people who might pay attention to you.

   You must also look at how people who read your ads might be sensitive to your content. You don't want to turn people off of certain things.

3. Compare the context of your message to the content you might exclude.

   Is your content relevant to sexually-sensitive or descriptive videos or articles? It might be best to exclude those from your content.

Chapter 43 – A/B Testing

As you work on AdWords, you will start to notice that certain ads might do a little better than others. Maybe those ads are working because you're using the correct keywords. Perhaps some ads are best because they include emotional words or calls to action that cause people to be more likely to respond.

What if you have no idea about what to get out of your ads? Maybe you have some useful ideas, but you are not certain about which ad will work. You don't have to stress out over this; you can use A/B testing to decide which ads are best for your marketing campaign.

A/B testing is comparing two different ads – Ad A and Ad B.

Testing your ads regularly helps you identify how well your campaign is being run and what you can expect to get out of it. By using the right testing plans, you will get the most out of your content and make what you are offering more viable and attractive to readers.

The process for A/B testing:

1. Go to the campaign listing on your AdWords page.

2. Select a campaign that you will use to create a draft.

    The draft is a new version of the campaign that you will run as a test. This will be compared with the old campaign to see how well each choice is run.

3. Select a new draft. This is what the test will use.

4. Enter a name for the draft.

5. Select a series of changes that you will make to the campaign.

6. Activate the draft as an experiment.

You will be given the option to do this. The listing should also include the option to update your original campaign with the new parameters. You can use the changes in your campaign later if you wish.

The process will help you understand what might work in your campaign if managed right. You can use the testing process as long as necessary, but you should only do this working when you are certain that you have a good plan for making your campaign stand out and run properly.

Chapter 44 – Checking Analytics (and Linking Google Analytics)

The Analytics of your AdWords campaign will make a big difference in how well your content is being handled. When you use the right Analytics points on AdWords, you will fully understand what you are getting from your efforts.

Campaign Analytics

As you review the Analytics on your dashboard, you will notice many features. The first section involves your campaign. The following sections are the key part of your campaign Analytics reports:

- The number of impressions you are getting from your ads

- How many interactions people are making with your ads

- The interaction rate

- The average cost of the clicks people are completing

- The total cost of your campaign

Ad Group Analytics

The ad groups that you are working with should be reviewed as well. The Analytics include:

- The default maximum CPC involved

- The targeted CPA that you want to use

- The general standards for the ad rotation

- The impressions and interactions that are occurring

- The costs involved

Linking Google Analytics

Google Analytics will give you up-to-the-minute information on how well your campaign is running. Specifically, you will find information on your AdWords campaign and how your customers act after getting onto your site from an AdWords link.

To link Google Analytics to your account:

1. Apply for an account with Google Analytics before you start doing anything.

   Your Analytics account will help you to get online fast and effectively.

2. Go to the Linked Accounts section of your AdWords account.

3. Click on the Google Analytics section.

4. Click to set up a link between your Analytics account and your AdWords account.

5. Import the site metrics that you have saved on Analytics to your AdWords page.

   Review how Google Analytics works and see how many fields you can add.

6. Click to Save the options.

After this is done, the Analytics information will appear throughout your AdWords account. Be aware of the Analytics support you get from AdWords.

Chapter 45 – Finding Special AdWords Deals

Many websites will offer special offers for people to get credits for Google AdWords. These include specials where people might get a certain amount of money to use on AdWords.

For example, you might have a desire to move your website to a certain hosting service provider. One incentive that provider might give you is $100 in free credits that you can use on AdWords. This is an attractive bonus that gives you extra freedom for how you are going to get your AdWords campaign to work out right.

As appealing as this might be, you have to be aware of some terms associated with any special AdWords deal. Each offer will have some limits. After all, that old idiom about something being "too good to be true" is indeed true.

Review the Minimums

You might have to adjust your AdWords campaign to take advantage of a special deal. For instance, you might get $100 in free credits to use on AdWords, but you might have to increase the total amount of money you will spend per day. You might have to hold a maximum budget of at least $10 or $20 a day to get those free credits. In short, you are not going to just get free credits that you can pocket and use by spreading them out over an extended period of time.

How Can You Use the Credits?

You might have limits on how your credits can be used. You could be told that you can only use your credits on specific types of campaigns or on particular bids. Know the rules that accompany the free credits.

Analyze Contracts

You might only be allowed to get those free AdWords credits if you sign up for a contract for services from some online provider. These include services for hosting a site or getting a domain name. The added expenses involved might be high. You might also have to stay in a contract for a year or longer before you can get out and consider other services.

When Are the Credits Available?

You might not get your credits as soon as you wish either. You might be limited to only getting your credits after a few weeks. This means you would have to spend regular money on your AdWords work before getting those credits. This is not always something that everyone is going to want to do.

Chapter 46 – Cancelling AdWords

Although AdWords might be appealing, it is understandable if you need to delete certain campaigns or ad groups or even cancel AdWords altogether.

Deleting Ad Groups or Campaigns

The process for eliminating an ad group or campaign is easy:

1. Click on the campaign or ad group you want to remove while on the layout.

   You can select just one or you can choose as many as you wish. If you do select a campaign, you will delete all the ad groups that link to that campaign at the same time it is removed.

2. Go to the Edit menu.

3. Click on the option to remove or delete the campaign or group. This should be marked by a red button.

   After this, the content will be fully removed from your AdWords account.

Note: Once you delete a group or campaign, you cannot bring it back. Be extremely cautious when deleting an entry, especially if you have a campaign with lots of ad groups.

Closing Your AdWords Account

There are many reasons why you might need to close your AdWords account. You might want to move on to some other advertising venture and you feel you no longer have a need for AdWords. Perhaps AdWords did not work for you, although the instructions in this book should have helped. There might also be an issue that your business can no longer afford AdWords.

To close your AdWords account:

1. Make sure you are the Admin area of your account.

2. Click on the tool icon.

3. Go to Preferences and then Account Status.

4. Select to cancel your account.

5. Make sure you review your credit or bank account statement after canceling. You will have to pay anything that you still owe after you cancel your account. You will still have access to your AdWords account by logging in. You just will not have the ability to create or use any ads.

6. If you have any credits left in your account, they will be refunded to your credit card or bank account via a wire transfer. Be advised that it might take a few weeks for the refund to be processed.

Reactivating an Account

You might need to reactivate your AdWords account. The financial situation of your business could have improved so you can return to using AdWords. Perhaps you have read more on AdWords and want to give it a second try.

To reactivate your AdWords account:

1. Log into your AdWords account.

2. Go to the tool section.

3. Get to the Preferences menu and then the Account Status section.

4. Select the option to reactivate your account.

It might take some time to get this back up, but you will be able to get back to your account at this point. Make sure you check the settings and that everything you are using is fully active and ready to work once again.

Conclusion

If there is one thing that can be said about Google AdWords, it is a truly impressive and distinct solution that works wonders for marketing. AdWords gives you a great setup for handling your marketing efforts and makes it easy for you to highlight whatever it is you are offering.

You will be impressed with how easily quality ads can be prepared when you get your AdWords campaign running and working well. You can do many things with a campaign when you know how it all works and you understand what you will get from your efforts.

Your AdWords campaign can work with numerous attractive features including the right keywords and memorable descriptions, videos, and other features.

You can use many types of ads when you are working with AdWords. The choices you have are extensive and can include everything from fine quality video ads to ads on a shopping section.

AdWords gives your campaigns functionality and gives you control over the kinds of ads you want to create. You should also think about what you will spend on your ads while looking at keywords and even how your landing pages are laid out. The extensive work involved should be explored in detail to see what makes your campaign so valuable.

Good luck with your Google AdWords endeavor. You will discover when working on AdWords that your campaign will stand out and have a special layout. If there is one thing that your site deserves, it is the ability to be noticed by as many people as possible.

Author's Note

Thank you for reading this book.

If you found this book to be useful, would you please write a positive review on Amazon?

I would greatly appreciate it.

Thanks again.

Made in the USA
Middletown, DE
24 January 2020